RACISM, AFRICAN AMERICANS, AND SOCIAL JUSTICE

Rudolph Alexander Jr.

ROWMAN & LITTLEFIELD PUBLISHERS, INC.
Lanham • Boulder • New York • Toronto • Oxford

ROWMAN & LITTLEFIELD PUBLISHERS, INC.

Published in the United States of America
by Rowman & Littlefield Publishers, Inc.
A wholly owned subsidiary of The Rowman & Littlefield Publishing Group, Inc.
4501 Forbes Boulevard, Suite 200, Lanham, MD 20706
www.rowmanlittlefield.com

P.O. Box 317, Oxford OX2 9RU, UK

British Library Cataloguing in Publication Information Available

Library of Congress Cataloging-in-Publication Data
Alexander, Rudolph.
  Racism, African Americans, and social justice / Rudolph Alexander, Jr.
      p. cm.
  Includes bibliographical references and index.
  ISBN 0-7425-4348-X (cloth : alk. paper) — ISBN 0-7425-4349-8 (pbk. : alk. paper)
  1. African Americans—Civil rights. 2. African Americans—Social conditions. 3.
African Americans—Legal status, laws, etc. 4. Racism—United States. 5. Race
discrimination—United States. 6. Social justice—United States. 7. United States—
Race relations. I. Title. E185.615.A623 2005
  305.896'073—dc22
                        2004024563

Printed in the United States of America

♾™ The paper used in this publication meets the minimum requirements of American
National Standard for Information Sciences—Permanence of Paper for Printed Library
Materials, ANSI/NISO Z39.48-1992.

RACISM, AFRICAN AMERICANS, AND SOCIAL JUSTICE

Contents

Preface

THE PRIMARY THESIS OF THIS BOOK is that justice is meted out less frequently to African Americans as compared to other races. While many people believe that the race problem in this country has been solved, race and racism continue to exist. For example, the U.S. Supreme Court decided two affirmative action cases in 2003. Also, one social scientist conducted a multivariate study with a national probability sample that examined the public attitudes about affirmative action, with the researcher concluding that "modern racism" existed among Whites. Then, there are always stories that emerge, such as some Cracker Barrel restaurants permitting waitresses to switch tables because they did not want to serve African Americans and referring to some sections in the restaurant where African Americans are seated as the "ghetto." Also, an African American anesthesiologist was removed from the operating room at a White husband's objection because the husband did not want the anesthesiologist to possibly see his wife naked on the operating table. The hospital later apologized to the anesthesiologist. In 2004, a Louisiana judge was suspended because he went to a costume party wearing chains and an Afro wig. Frequently, incidents such as that which occurred at the Cracker Barrel restaurants, the hospital, and the party are publicized, causing many African Americans to wonder what else is occurring away from the public eye.

In addition, many African Americans and Whites see events differently, making a meeting of the minds more difficult and challenging forward progress. The O. J. Simpson saga typifies that African Americans and Whites differ in how they see events and process these events. Differences were shown in how each group saw the O. J. Simpson criminal and civil verdicts.

Even interpretations of African Americans' behavior are seen through a racial prism.

A frequently shown scene that invited negative comments by Whites was the view of an auditorium of law students at Howard University jumping up and cheering when the criminal verdict in the O. J. Simpson case was announced. Numerous Whites saw the students' behaviors as celebrating a corrupt verdict that freed a guilty killer. Another interpretation of those students' behaviors, which few White persons saw, was that it was a celebration of a win by an African American attorney in a lead position—a scene seldom viewed in this country. Those African American law students probably had not been born the last time an African American attorney won an acquittal in a major case—the case of Angela Davis in the 1970s. Thus, while many Whites saw the students as cheering for O. J. Simpson, some African Americans, including myself, saw them as African Americans cheering for an African American attorney winning a major, major case.

Moreover, many African Americans and Whites differ regarding the extent to which they believe that race impinges upon American institutions. Typically, African Americans believe race is more of a factor in American society than Whites do. Some Whites believe that race is not much of a factor in contemporary society and that charges of racism made by African Americans are disingenuous, indicating an attempt to exploit a situation for personal promotion or "playing the race card." Whatever racism that has existed in society has been long gone, according to many Whites. Furthermore, some social commentators state that racial advancement, as it applies to African Americans, has been tremendous, tacitly marking slavery as the beginning and comparing that period to contemporary society.

This book acknowledges that, indeed, improvement in racial interaction has occurred, but significant issues still remain. Issues remain in education, employment, social justice, and the legal system. This book delineates the contours of how African Americans receive less justice in several areas. This book updates and expands upon an earlier book that was published in 2000 on race and justice and has been broadened to include revisions of all chapters, three additional chapters, and a summarizing chapter. The three new chapters discuss justice issues in the military, economics, and reparations.

Chapter 1 begins with a discussion of the history of race and justice, laying the roots for a double standard that negatively applies to descendants of Africans even to this day. The animus shown toward African Americans is unparalleled in comparison to other groups in America. While the history of race issues, such as the Dred Scott case, is given, all chapters begin with some historical context to the problem. This chapter discusses how Whites in the early 1900s used the principle of being "colorblind" to deprive African Americans of the right to vote and how conservative Whites today are championing a current "colorblind" society.

Chapter 2 discusses African Americans and higher education. A popular belief among many Whites is that African Americans are being given seats in universities that should go to higher-scoring Whites. What is often overlooked is that some White students with average and sometimes below-average scores have no problem getting into universities, but no one has accused these lower-scoring White students of taking seats from higher-scoring White students. The focus is always put upon a few African American students. This chapter also discusses the two cases involving affirmative action and the University of Michigan that the U.S. Supreme Court decided in 2003.

Chapter 3 discusses African Americans and the juvenile justice system. It discusses the myth that African American juveniles are slapped on the wrist and contends that the perspective that juveniles are handled leniently by the justice system does not apply to African American juveniles. Since the creation of the first juvenile court in 1899, African American juveniles have been handled by the adult system and frequently they have been executed or sent to adult prisons with lengthy sentences. More times than not, the cases were dubious and trials were held in record time. Currently, African American youth are incarcerated in high numbers for drugs—a fate not reserved for White juveniles. This revised chapter adds a study in how White and African American juveniles are assessed differently by White probation officers.

Chapter 4 discusses African Americans and law enforcement. This chapter on law enforcement and race challenges the popular explanation of why African Americans are stopped more frequently than Whites. The popular explanation is that African Americans are more likely to be involved in serious criminal activity, and this high criminal involvement justifies or explains why law enforcement interacts more with them than other racial groups. This chapter provides statistics that show, for instance, that Whites steal more automobiles than African Americans. Accordingly, Whites should be stopped at random for proof of registration, but this is not done. The same applies to drugs. A significant number of Whites possess and use drugs and do so more than African Americans, but Whites are not targeted for stops.

Chapter 5 discusses African Americans in the military. One of the first persons to be killed in the skirmish that sparked the American Revolutionary War was an African American seaman. Slaves were sometimes sent to war to serve for the slaveholders and the slaveholders received money and land as a result of their slaves' service. African American soldiers participated and died in every military engagement, and their service to this country has gone unnoticed and unappreciated. Currently, African Americans constitute the largest minority group serving in the military, far surpassing Latinos, who are now the largest minority group in the United States. African American women make up almost half of the women in the military presently. This chapter, consistent with the theme of African Americans receiving less justice, discusses the issue of Jessica Lynch, whom Whites tried to make a national heroine while ignoring Shoshana Johnson, an African American soldier who was shot and injured in the same convoy in which Jessica Lynch was injured.

Chapter 6 discusses African Americans and economic discrimination. This chapter discusses the struggle with African Americans' trying to make strides economically but being impeded by racism that continues presently. It relates how land, a form of wealth, was taken from African Americans illegally and legally, and buying houses and lots was made more difficult for them for years. Then, discrimination has also occurred in the banking and insurance industries. For instance, the U.S. government created the practice of "redlining," in which loans would not be given in poor or African American neighborhoods. In 2003, two large automobile manufacturers with affiliations with financing companies agreed to discontinue their racist practice of charging African Americans more for car loans than Whites. These practices have had the effect of draining African Americans economically.

Chapter 7 discusses African Americans and reparations. This new chapter outlines the history and arguments for and against reparations. It discusses the Jews receiving reparations from Germany and several Swiss banks, and Japanese Americans receiving reparations from the U.S. government for the Japanese American internment in camps during World War II. It counters a racist critic who contends that African Americans are racists for discussing reparations and that African Americans have already received reparations in the form of welfare and affirmative action. However, more Whites receive public assistance than African Americans. During the third presidential debate between President Bush and Senator John Kerry, Senator Kerry stressed that affirmative action has benefited women and not just African Americans. In fact, some data show that White women have benefited the most from affirmative action. Further, this chapter discusses the case involving reparations for slavery that was dismissed in federal court in 2004.

Chapter 8 discusses African Americans, discrimination, and legal justice. In law, the legal standard to decide discrimination cases disfavors African Americans. The current legal standard that African Americans must achieve is almost impossible because the standard requires, in part, the disproving of a subjective factor. For instance, if an employer states that a job was given to a White person because this person interviewed better than an African American candidate, this subjective component cannot be disproved. Thus, the African American plaintiff loses. As one judge stated, a disparity between an African American and white candidate must jump up and slap judges in the face in order for an African American plaintiff to prevail in a lawsuit. Further, this chapter adds discussions of a study that concludes that modern racism exists against African Americans.

Chapter 9 is a summary of key aspects of the chapters and concluding remarks.

In many of these chapters, I discuss legal cases. Most of these cases are from the federal system. There are three levels of the federal judicial system, consisting of the U.S. district court, courts of appeals, and the U.S. Supreme Court. The U.S. district court is a trial court. So, a racial or sex discrimination case based on federal law begins at this level. Next is the court of appeals, consisting of twelve courts of appeal, which include the D.C. Circuit. Each court of appeals covers a number of states in its circuit, and a ruling is binding on all states in that circuit. For instance, Texas, Louisiana, and Mississippi are in the Fifth Circuit Court of Appeals. Georgia, Florida, and Alabama are in the Eleventh Circuit Court of Appeals. In the federal system, the courts of appeal are particularly important because the U.S. Supreme Court does not hear all the cases that come to it. More times than not, a federal appeal ends at the court of appeals level because the U.S. Supreme Court frequently lets a court of appeals ruling stand without a review.

1

African Americans and Justice: An Introduction

A̲FRICAN AMERICANS DIFFER FROM White Americans in assessing the amount of racial discrimination in society (Wilson, 1973). Typically, African Americans opine that discrimination is much more rampant than what White Americans indicate (The Gallup Organization, 1997). African Americans believe that they suffer from discrimination economically and socially. For instance, in 1997, African Americans reported experiencing discrimination while shopping, dining out, encountering the police, at work, and using public transportation (The Gallup Organization, 1997). African Americans examine statistics regarding their high imprisonment rate, lower income, lower positions in companies, and higher mortality rates, suggesting that these are indices of social and economic discrimination. This view indicates discrimination in employment, housing, education, economics, and the courts (The Gallup Organization, 1997). Stated differently, African Americans believe that they receive less justice than other groups.

On the other hand, White Americans attribute African Americans' status to problematic values and excessive reliance on government (Murray, 1984). Further, they indicate that discrimination against African Americans does not exist, or any discrimination that may exist is minuscule (Wilbanks, 1987). Moreover, many White Americans believe that African Americans' charges of racism are disingenuous and are attempts to excuse failure or to extract undeserved rewards. In fact, White Americans have coined a phrase to describe this view, calling it "playing the race card" (Beck, 1998; Ellerton, 1998; Mooney, 1998; Muwakkil, 1998), a term made more popular in the criticisms of attorney Johnny Cochran and his defense of O. J. Simpson. Since then, whenever many African Americans contend that they have been impacted by racism, it is described as "playing the race card."

White Americans frequently imply that something is wrong with African Americans, pointing out how other groups have prospered in this country without protective legislation, such as Italian Americans, Irish Americans, Jewish Americans, and Asian Americans (Herrnstein & Murray, 1994). However, these comparisons are invalid. While discrimination did exist at one time against these groups, and some discrimination and prejudice still exists, such as anti-Semitism, the quality of this discrimination is different from what African Americans have experienced and are now experiencing.

Principally, these groups did not have Jim Crow laws to fight, and they were not subjected to the degree of violence and oppression that African Americans experienced (Belknap, 1987). These groups (i.e., the Irish, Jews, and Italians) tended to settle on the northeastern coast when they came to America. There is no record of these groups being legally denied education, voting, and becoming naturalized citizens; being lynched; or having to contend with the Ku Klux Klan with no protection from legal authorities.

Further, Italian Americans, Irish Americans, and Jewish Americans are viewed as Caucasians too, which provides them with a measure of inclusion. For instance, a federal district court in California, differentiating Chinese and others groups, referred to "our worthy resident aliens from Europe—gentlemen of Irish or German nativity" (*In re Quong Woo*, 1882, p. 30). Moreover, these groups could easily escape some discrimination by changing their names or just blending in with the dominant European group. As an illustration, in a region where virulent discrimination existed, Jewish Americans, Irish Americans, and Italian Americans could eat in a restaurant, and no one would know who they were. But African Americans would be quickly recognized when entering a restaurant. In effect, skin color is a barrier to some discrimination. Asians, especially the Chinese in the nineteenth century, suffered some discrimination, but other Asians within the last twenty-five years have come to America when discrimination had abated, hateful attitudes had softened, and effective civil rights laws existed.

Among minority groups in the United States, African Americans occupy the most unique position of all groups. African Americans were the only group to be brought to America involuntarily and enslaved for hundreds of years. Shortly after the end of slavery, the Black Codes were passed, which were a series of laws to control African Americans. Later, other laws were passed to prevent African Americans from voting, serving on juries, or moving into certain neighborhoods. This history suggests that Whites feared and disliked African Americans more than any other minority group (Jordan, 1968). For instance, the U.S. Supreme Court, in upholding the segregation of private colleges, stated that laws forbidding intermarriages, preventing the offspring of interracial parents from inheriting, separating races in educational institutions, and separating races on public transportation had one common purpose: "to preserve race identity, the purity of blood, and prevent an amalgamation" (*Berea College v. Kentucky*, 1908, p. 51).

Without a doubt, the degree of oppression and discrimination against African Americans has abated (Wilson, 1980). However, significant discriminatory practices and policies still exist (Poe, 1998). As evidence, one needs only to examine stories involving major corporations in America. Nationwide Insurance, a large company based in Columbus, Ohio, has been found guilty of discriminating against minorities, mostly African Americans, in providing insurance coverage and ordered to pay $100 million in damages (Dugas, 1998). After an appeal, Nationwide agreed to settle the case for $17.5 million, and officials disclosed that Nationwide has settled several similar lawsuits (Porter, 2000). Wendy's, a restaurant chain, has been accused of discrimination by preferring Whites who want to buy franchises over African Americans who want to buy franchises.

While these businesses deny that they have engaged in discrimination, several executives from Texaco were secretly recorded spewing their animosity toward African Americans (Bryant, 1998). Although these executives were acquitted of destroying evidence, the Texaco Corporation agreed to pay 1,300 African American employees $176 million (Poe, 1998). A broadcast on the television show *60 Minutes* described that pervasive and systematic discrimination by local farm service agencies has been practiced against African American farmers, prompting a class action lawsuit against the U.S. Department of Justice for not processing farmers' civil rights complaints (Atkinson, 1998). Also, the strategy of sending African Americans and Whites to renters and realtors to detect discrimination in housing shows still that some individuals will not sell or rent to African Americans (Parish, 1998; Walker, 1997), and some realtors steer African Americans away from certain neighborhoods (Garrett, 1997; Mayer, 1997). In New York City, Representative Charles Schumer reported that among African Americans, Hispanics, and Whites with equal income, African Americans were more likely to be rejected for home loans by banks ("Widespread Redlining Exposed," 1998). Recently, the U.S. Supreme Court has been criticized for its current hiring practices with respect to law clerks. The present Court has hired 428 clerks. Of this total, 75 percent were males and 25 percent were females. Racially, only 1.6 percent were African Americans (Mauro, 1998). Further, the current chief justice of the U.S. Supreme Court, William Rehnquist, was rebuked for leading judges at a conference in the singing of "Dixie," a song praising slavery times (Rankin, 1999; Timberg, 1999). These examples and illustrations from the 1990s show that race and justice remain a considerable issue.

This introductory chapter argues that African Americans still experience significant discrimination in a number of areas and have a more difficult time receiving justice as the millennium begins. To understand why, it is necessary to define and explain what justice is and then to trace the lack of justice for African Americans beginning with their arrival in America, the attitudes and behaviors of White society as slavery ended, the use of laws to oppress African Americans, differential interpretation of laws depending upon race and ethnicity, and the relevance of the past to the present. In developing these areas, this chapter relies considerably upon court decisions for two reasons. First, courts often provide leadership to society, indicating right and wrong and just and unjust. As such, the courts are instrumental in deciding justice. Equally important, court decisions provide a rich source of historical information that is readily obtainable. Many times, court decisions provide specific state statutes and provide an historical account of laws and legislatures' will.

Explanations of Justice, Social Justice, and Economic Justice

Aristotle discussed justice and explained justice indirectly by saying that people should desist from pleonexia, which means gaining some advantage for themselves by seizing that which belongs to others. These advantages could be property, reward, or office. Justice also involves denying persons that which is due them, such as the fulfillment of a promise, the repayment of debt, and the showing of proper respect (Rawls, 1971).

Similar to Aristole, Bernard Vincent Brady (1998) explains justice by considering injustice. When individuals experience injustice, it induces strong emotions, such as anger, rage, and bitterness. Further, injustice has negative consequences in that it damages and fractures relationships. Brady (1998) identified five types of justice—interpersonal justice, commutative justice, distributive justice, communal justice, and social justice. Interpersonal justice involves the responsibilities that individuals have with close interpersonal intimates, such as friends and families. Commutative justice entails those responsibilities to others based on professional, employment, and business relationships. Distributive justice involves society's responsibility through the government to allocate resources and burdens fairly. Communal justice consists of individuals, groups, and organizations within society pursuing and promoting the common good. Social justice is the responsibility of individuals to advance the well-being of the vulnerable (i.e., the powerless, the poor, the sick, the aged, children, crime victims, and prisoners), particularly by the critique of the social structure and social institutions.

According to John Rawls (1971), the first virtue of social institutions is justice. Each person has an inviolability based on justice and even the welfare of society cannot supersede it. Justice, for this reason, rejects the principle that the loss of freedom for some is made right by a greater good for others. Justice "does not allow that the sacrifices imposed on a few are outweighed by the larger sum of advantages enjoyed by many" (p. 4). Justice comes into issue whenever there is an allotment of anything rationally regarded as disadvantageous or advantageous. Rawls asserts that society is a self-sufficient association of individuals who in their relation with each other generally accept that rules are binding and try to adhere to them. Nevertheless, there is a conflict of interest among individuals because these individuals are aware of the distribution of benefits that are produced by them. A set of principles is necessary for deciding among the various social arrangements that decide this allotment of advantages and for endorsing an agreement on the fair distributive shares. The name for these aforementioned principles is social justice.

A simpler understanding of justice may be found in *Webster's Ninth New Collegiate Dictionary* (1985) and the *Social Work Dictionary*. Webster's dictionary defines justice as the maintenance and administration of what is just especially by the impartial adjustment of conflicting claims or the assignment of merited rewards and punishments. It is also the quality of being just, impartial, or fair. To do justice means to act justly, to treat fairly or adequately, and to show due appreciation for. Similarly, the *Social Work Dictionary* defines justice as the principle of fairness and equity, especially in accordance with moral and ethical rightness, social standards, and law. Also, social justice is an ideal condition in which all members of a society have the same basic rights, protection, opportunities, obligations, and social benefits. Implicit in this concept is the notion that historical inequalities should be acknowledged and remedied through specific measures. A key social work value, social justice entails advocacy to confront discrimination, oppression, and institutional inequities. Last, social work defines economic justice as a condition in which all members of society have the same opportunities to obtain material resources necessary to survive and fulfill their human potential (Barker, 2003, p. 137).

Attitudes of Whites about African Americans near the End of Slavery and After Slavery

In *Dred Scott v. Sandford* (1856), the U.S. Supreme Court grappled with the issue of whether Dred Scott, a person of African descent, was a citizen and could sue in the courts. In a very lengthy decision that consisted of 240 pages, the Court ruled that no person of African descent, even those who had been freed or thought that they had been freed, was a citizen of the United States. (Most U.S. Supreme Court decisions consist of twenty or thirty pages, and a lengthy decision may be fifty or sixty pages.) In reaching this decision, the Court gave a lengthy recitation of why Africans were not citizens, a position, the majority stated, that was shared by the U.S. Attorney General, the U.S. Secretary of State, Congress, and the thirteen original states. Moreover, all the important documents, such as the Declaration of Independence and the U.S. Constitution, as well as federal and state statutes supported the view that people of African descent were not citizens or intended to be citizens.

Justice Benjamin Curtis, who wrote the majority opinion and was formerly a prominent attorney in Massachusetts, made numerous derogatory statements in his opinion that he declared that *all* White persons endorsed. Referring to Africans, Justice Curtis wrote:

> They had for more than a century before been regarded as beings of an inferior order, and altogether unfit to associate with the White race, either in social or political relations; and so far inferior, that they had no rights which the White man was bound to respect; and that the negro might justly and lawfully be reduced to slavery for his benefit. He was bought and sold, and treated as an ordinary article of merchandise and traffic, whenever a profit could be made by it. This opinion was at that time fixed and universal in the civilized portion of the White race. It was regarded as an axiom in morals as well as in politics, which no one thought of disputing, or supposed to be open [sic] to dispute; and men in every grade and position in society daily and habitually acted upon it in their private pursuits, as well as in matters of public concern, without doubting for a moment the correctness of this opinion. (*Dred Scott v. Sandford*, 1856, p. 407)

Justice Curtis observed that even states that were opponents of slavery passed laws forbidding Africans from marrying Whites, such as Massachusetts, Connecticut, New Hampshire, and Rhode Island. In describing Rhode Island's prohibition against intermarriages, Justice Curtis wrote that "down to the last-mentioned period, the strongest mark of inferiority and degradation was fastened upon the African race" (*Dred Scott v. Sandford*, 1856, p. 416). New Hampshire passed a law restricting the militia to free White citizens, which was reported to indicate that "nothing could more strongly mark the entire repudiation of the African race" (p. 415). Connecticut was the first state to end slavery in its state and passed a law forbidding the importation of slaves in its state. But, according to Justice Curtis, the Connecticut legislation did not indicate "any change of opinion as to the relative rights and position of the white and black races in this country, or indicating that it meant to place the latter, when free, upon a level with its citizens" (p. 413). In no part of the country, except Maine, were African Americans permitted to participate equally with Whites in the exercise of civil and political rights (*Dred Scott v. Sandford,* 1856).

Justice John Harlan, dissenting in the infamous *Plessy v. Ferguson* case, observed that attitudes toward African Americans were affected by the institution of slavery. He observed that in many localities public opinion was so dominated by slavery that "it would not have been safe to do justice to the Black man; and when, so far as the rights of blacks were concerned, race prejudice was, practically the supreme law of the land" (*Plessy v. Ferguson,* 1896, p. 563).

In the South, Southerners resented the forced political gains of African Americans during the Reconstruction period that followed the South losing the Civil War (Clark, 1973). As a justice of the Supreme Court of Mississippi wrote, "our unhappy state had passed in rapid succession from civil war through a period of military occupancy, followed by another, in which the control of public affairs had passed to a recently enfranchised race, unfitted by educational experience for the responsibility thrust upon it. This was succeeded by a semimilitary, semicivil uprising, under which the White race inferior in number, but superior in spirit, in governmental instinct, and in intelligence, was restored to power" (*Ratliff v. Beale,* 1896, p. 867).

These views and thoughts provided a precarious position for African Americans in this country. During slavery, African Americans were forbidden from learning to read and write. After slavery, some laws were passed to protect the rights of African Americans, such as the Fourteenth Amendment and the Civil Rights Act of 1871. But these federal laws were mostly ineffective. Most states successfully maneuvered around these laws, and often it was the U.S. Supreme Court providing support for the principle of white supremacy.

The Use of Law to Oppress African Americans

In contemporary society, individuals look to the law to redress grievances and view it as a vehicle for righting wrongs. Derrick Bell (1980), however, indicated that this view has not been correct historically and that the law has been used as an instrument of oppression with respect to African Americans. To illustrate, the supreme law of a state or country is its constitution. Written broadly, it is of superior and paramount force, unlike a state or federal statute. When a statute conflicts with the constitution, it is the statute that must yield (*Ratliff v. Beale,* 1896). Hence, a constitution is the supreme law of a state and country. Thus, it follows that one way to provide advantage to some individuals and disadvantage to other individuals is through the creation of a constitution or changes in a constitution. This was done by a number of states (*Guinn and Beal v. United States,* 1915; *Myers et al. v. Anderson,* 1915).

During the Reconstruction period, African Americans held political offices and voted throughout the South. The perception of many White Southerners was that African Americans had not earned these privileges. As a result, African Americans should abandon these rights and privileges until they were educationally prepared to vote and hold political offices (Clark, 1973). But in reality, this time would never come in many White persons' eyes.

When Reconstruction ended, the South sought to ensure that white supremacy reigned in the states. Mississippi was in the vanguard of creating a constitution that protected white supremacy, and a number of other states followed Mississippi's lead. Guided by the Mississippi Plan, the Mississippi Constitution of 1890 had four key parts aimed at disenfranchising African Americans. These were found in Section 241, which involved crimes that disqualified individuals from voting; Section 242, which involved the registration process; Section 243, which involved the paying of poll taxes in order to vote; and Section 244, which involved literacy requirements in order to vote (Clark, 1973). While poor Whites were affected too by these elements, their disenfranchisement was a by-product of or secondary to the original plan to ensure the oppression of African Americans. At that time, African Americans were in the majority in terms of numbers and the aim was to eliminate virtually all of them from voting. If African Americans could not vote, they could not affect the political system or improve their lives.

The justices of the Supreme Court of Mississippi were quite frank in the intent of the framers of the Mississippi Constitution of 1890. This intent of White Mississippians was reported in a decision involving a dispute over poll taxes. The case involved whether a sheriff was justified in seizing property to satisfy poll taxes and specifically what was meant by the word "lien" in the Mississippi Constitution. To ascertain the meaning of lien, the justices stated that they had to look to the body of law, the old constitution, the purposes to be accomplished, and the "existing evils." The court noted that "we are to consider the condition of things as existing at the time, and especially must we note those grave and permeating forces for evil which were known by all men to exist, the silent and increasing influences of which were corrupting the public conscience, and threatening to involve in common ruin the morals and civilization of one race, and the liberty and safety of another" (*Ratliff v. Beale*, 1896, p. 867). The court stated that "the difficulty, as all men knew, arose from racial differences" (*Ratliff v. Beale*, 1896, p. 867).

At that time, Congress had passed the Fourteenth Amendment to the U.S. Constitution, which states, in part, that all individuals are citizens and no state shall deprive any person of life, liberty, or property without due process of law. As the U.S. Supreme Court interpreted it, the Fourteenth Amendment's "main purpose was to establish the citizenship of the negro; to give definitions of citizenship of the United States and of the States; and to protect from the hostile legislation of the States the privileges and immunities of citizens of the United States, as distinguished from those of citizens of the States" (*Plessy v. Ferguson*, 1896, p. 543).

The Mississippi Plan recognized that there were limitations put upon states by virtue of the Fourteenth Amendment, but "within the field of permissible action under the limitations imposed by the federal constitution, the convention swept the circle of expedients to obstruct the exercise of the franchise by the negro race" (*Ratliff v. Beale*, 1896, p. 868). The justices noted that African Americans were different than Whites in that African Americans were "careless, landless, and migratory . . . [and their] criminal members given rather to furtive offenses than to the robust crimes of the Whites" (p. 868). So, crimes such as burglary, theft, arson, and obtaining money under false pretenses were disqualifying crimes because they were thought to be committed more by African Americans, but robbery and murder were not disqualifying because these were the types of crimes most committed by Whites. Because White Mississippians could not discriminate against African Americans through explicit laws, "the convention discriminated against the characteristics and the offenses to which its weaker members were prone" (*Ratliff v. Beale*, 1896, p. 868).

One of the key issues in *Ratliff* was whether the poll tax was principally a revenue measure for schools or a device to keep African Americans from voting. The court stated that "in our opinion, the clause was primarily intended by the framers of the constitution as a clog upon the franchise, and secondarily and incidentally only as a means of revenue" (*Ratliff v. Beale*, 1896, p. 869). In other words, the poll tax principally was to prevent African Americans from voting.

Although the Mississippi Constitution had a clear intent to oppress African Americans, this fact was subsequently ignored. In 1896, the Supreme Court of Mississippi said that race was a primary factor in the creation of the poll tax. But two years later, the same Mississippi court ruled that race was not an issue in how an African American went on trial for killing a White man with an all-White jury drawn from the same poll tax list (*Williams v. Mississippi*, 1898). The U.S. Supreme Court equally ignored this racial intent in upholding a murder conviction of this African American defendant (*Williams v. Mississippi*, 1898). The Williams decision reflected a pattern of how judges and justices capriciously interpreted the law when race and justice were involved.

In 1998, the Fifth Circuit Court of Appeals revisited the Mississippi Constitution. A Mississippi prisoner, who was serving time for armed robbery, sued to vote, contending that the Mississippi Constitution did not specifically bar him from voting. The Mississippi Constitution bars people from voting who have been convicted of theft, but did not say anything about armed robbery. In addition, this prisoner contended that the choice of crimes listed in the

Mississippi Constitution had a racist origin. The judges on the Fifth Circuit acknowledged that the original crimes listed were to prevent African Americans from voting, but the judges stated that racism in the Mississippi Constitution was overcome by revisions in 1950 and 1968, which the people endorsed in elections. Specifically, murder and rape, considered to be White crimes that were originally excluded, were included. Accordingly, the racism in the Mississippi Constitution had been erased (*Brown v. Fordice*, 1998).

Contrary to what the Fifth Circuit judges wrote, the people of Mississippi did not cleanse their constitution in 1950 and 1968. First, few African Americans were permitted to vote in 1950 and 1968. Mississippi was the bastion for white supremacy and numerous African Americans had been killed for attempting to vote. A state-supported commission was created in the 1950s to prevent African Americans from voting and was supplying information to the Ku Klux Klan to carry out its plan to commit violence against African Americans seeking justice.

Capricious Interpretation of Laws and Leadership: Role of the Court

Contrary to the belief that laws provide stability in society and consistency can be found in their interpretations, many laws during the nineteenth century were broad in nature, permitting interpretations based on individuals' personal philosophies and interests. Often, African Americans did not receive justice, as judges shifted their positions. As an example, Kaczorowski (1985), a law professor, analyzed the role of U.S. Supreme Court Justice Joseph P. Bradley in curtailing civil rights enforcement during 1874 and 1875. According to Kaczorowski, a decision involving butchers in New Orleans "forced Bradley to change some of his earlier views concerning national civil rights enforcement authority" (Kaczorowski, 1985, p. 179). In a decision involving a change of venue for an African American defendant, Justice Bradley's opinion was said "to be riddled with contradiction" (Kaczorowski, 1985, p. 185) in ruling against the defendant.

In another example, Associate U.S. Supreme Court Justice John Campbell played a key role in denying congressional authority to prohibit slavery in the territories. In effect, he took a narrow view of congressional powers (Delaney, 1998). After leaving the U.S. Supreme Court, Justice Campbell became a lawyer in private practice. Returning to the Court, former Justice Campbell argued for a broad interpretation of the Fourteenth Amendment in representing the meat butchers in New Orleans, Louisiana. By a five-to-four margin, the Court ruled against the butchers, but one Justice expressed sympathy for the butchers' position (Delaney, 1998).

Still later, former Justice Campbell, representing a group of Whites, argued another case before the U.S. Supreme Court in 1876. The White men had been indicted under the Federal Enforcement Act of 1870 for killing sixty African Americans who were attempting to participate in the electoral process in Colfax, Louisiana, in what was called the Grant Parish massacre. In this case, Justice Campbell argued for a narrow interpretation of congressional powers. The Court agreed and threw out the indictments (Delaney, 1998). A few years later, the U.S. Supreme Court gave a broad interpretation of the Fourteenth Amendment and held that businesses were persons (*Minneapolis and St. Louis Railway Company v. Beckwith*, 1889), though this was not stated in the Fourteenth Amendment or the historical debate surrounding its enactment (James, 1984). In effect, race received one type of interpretation, and other issues received another type of interpretation. Even differences between races can be found in U.S. Supreme Court decisions, especially when African Americans were involved.

For instance, the U.S. Supreme Court ruled a San Francisco ordinance unconstitutional because it distinguished between laundries in wooden buildings and laundries in brick buildings (*Yick Wo v. Hopkins*, 1886). This case involved an attempt to oppress and discriminate against laundries operated and owned by Chinese. The Chinese laundries were in wooden buildings, and the White laundries were primarily in brick buildings. This ordinance was criminal in nature, and all the arrests, except one, were of Chinese. Although the ordinance never referred to Chinese, it was quite clear that the intent and purpose of the law was to oppress Chinese laundries. The Court ruled that even if a law is neutral in wording but officials apply the law with an evil eye and unequal hand so as to promote unjust and illegal discrimination for people who are similarly situated, then the disadvantaged group is denied equal justice (*Yick Wo v. Hopkins*, 1886).

However, African Americans were denied a similar ruling just ten years later when they encountered discrimination. As Justice Harlan stated in *Plessy v. Ferguson* (1896), African Americans fought to preserve the Union for the North, but they were not deemed to be citizens. But on the other hand, the Chinese, who could not be citizens either, were given more rights and justice than African Americans. With African Americans in Mississippi, the intent was to disenfranchise them because they were in the majority. Prior to the enactment of the Mississippi Constitution of 1890, 190,000 African Americans were qualified to vote and 69,000 Whites (*Williams v. Mississippi*, 1897). After enactment of the new Constitution with its poll tax, literary requirement, criminal convictions as a bar to voting, and registration process, the number of African Americans qualified to vote dropped to near zero. Yet, the U.S. Supreme Court refused to extend its ruling in *Yick Wo. v Hopkins* (1886) to

African Americans in *Plessy v. Ferguson* (1896) and *Williams v. Mississippi* (1897). Moreover, in a weak and ludicrous explanation and differentiation, the U.S. Supreme Court tried to assert that the Chinese were discriminated against in San Francisco, California, but African Americans were not in Mississippi.

Reflecting still the giving of less justice to African Americans than other groups, the U.S. Supreme Court upheld the conviction of Berea College, a private college in Kentucky, for educating Whites and African Americans together. The Kentucky legislature had passed a law with multiple sections to forbid colleges from educating African Americans and Whites, forbid a teacher from teaching African Americans and Whites, and forbid any African American or White from attending a college where the other race is. A college, however, could educate Whites and African Americans, but the sites had to be at least twenty-five miles apart. In dissent, Justice Harlan observed that if Kentucky could constitutionally pass such a law, it could forbid the association of Anglo-Saxon and Latin races or persons of the Christian and Jewish faith (*Berea College v. Kentucky*, 1908). The implication of Justice Harlan's statement is that only African Americans were targeted for separation, and if the Kentucky statute specifically referred to Latin races or Jewish persons for separation, the Court's view would have been different.

This type of differentiation reflects a pattern of rulings that favored other ethnic groups, especially if these groups were Caucasian. For instance, James E. Boyd, who was born in Ireland in 1834, came to the United States with his family in 1844. The family resided in Ohio, and Boyd's father became a U.S. citizen. The family later moved to Nebraska. James E. Boyd held several political offices in Nebraska and was subsequently elected Governor. After winning the governor's office, a dispute developed over whether Boyd was a citizen. The U.S. Supreme Court sided with Boyd with no derogatory reference to Boyd's Irish roots (*Boyd v. Nebraska*, 1892).

In another case involving Jews that hinted at anti-Semitism, the Cleveland Jewish Orphans' Home sought to build an orphanage on land that it owned. It was forbidden by the Village of University Heights from building, and the officials gave three reasons. First, the proposed land use would deny tax revenues to the municipality. Second, more children would need to be served by the educational system, requiring more resources. Third, the public welfare would not be served by having a group of children of the same race, creed, or nationality served by a single school. The U.S. district court enjoined the Village of University Heights from enforcing its ordinance and the Sixth Circuit Court of Appeals found the ordinance to be arbitrary and unreasonable (*Village of University Heights et al. v. Cleveland Jewish Orphans' Home*, 1927a). In addition, the U.S. Supreme Court refused to hear the case and thereby upheld the lower federal courts (*Village of University Heights et al. v. Cleveland Jewish Orphans' Home*, 1927b).

Justice in the Criminal Courts

Although a number of injustices against African Americans stand out, the criminal courts provide more glaring injustices. The current charge that Americans are soft on crime is neither reflective of history nor the present. African American males are the only group whose members have been executed for *attempted rape.* Often, these trials occurred at lighting speed. As an illustration, in Virginia attempted rape was punishable by the death penalty until the 1960s. A twenty-six-year-old African American male was sentenced to die for attempting to rape a seventeen-year-old White female. According to the woman, a man came up behind her and threw a rag over her head as she was walking to work on a country road. She could not identify the man and never saw him. The African American man lived near the woman and was interviewed. Reportedly, his story of his whereabouts did not check out, and he was interviewed again. Then, he was alleged to have confessed to the assault. This alleged assault occurred on December 8, 1920, and the indictment and trial occurred on December 9, 1920. The jury could not reach a verdict that day and tried to resolve the case the next day, December 10, 1920. A mistrial was declared and more jurors were summoned on December 10, 1920. A second trial occurred on December 11, 1920, and then the defendant was convicted and sentenced to die. In rejecting the condemned appeal, the Supreme Court of Virginia wrote that "the likelihood of the resort to lynch law, unless there is a prompt conviction and a severe penalty imposed, and thus a resultant grave shock to the peace and dignity of the Commonwealth is well known to exist" (*Hart v. Commonwealth*, 1921, p. 747). Although the Virginia court indicated that this was prompt justice, what, in fact, occurred was the railroading and legal lynching of an African American male.

In another case, a White female was alleged to have been raped by an African American male on May 17, 1931, in Elbert County, Georgia. On May 18, 1931, four African Americans were arrested and jailed as suspects. On May 19, 1931, two more African American males were arrested as suspects. All the suspects had to be transported out of town because a mob had gathered and threatened to lynch them all. On May 25, 1931, one defendant, John Downer, was indicted by the grand jury. Downer was tried, convicted, and sentenced to die the next day, May 26, 1931. The jury was out for five minutes, and Downer was scheduled to be executed on June 15, 1931. No appeal was filed in Downer's behalf before the Georgia appellate courts. Two days before

Downer's execution, a habeas corpus petition was filed in federal court, and a hearing was ordered held on whether Downer's rights had been violated (*Downer v. Dunaway*, 1932). These types of trial were the norm and were facilitated by the process existing during the time.

For instance, beatings and torture were routine practices in forcing African Americans to confess to crimes or to waive important rights. The conviction of an African American was reversed in Mississippi because he confessed after a severe beating. More importantly, the officers saw nothing wrong with their behavior and stated that beating criminal defendants to extract confessions was normal practice (*Brown v. Mississippi*, 1936). When physical beatings slowed in the criminal justice system, psychological torture was utilized, and often the defendants were uneducated or mentally challenged. For instance, an African American defendant, who had a third-grade education and had been diagnosed with schizophrenia, was given the death penalty for burglary and attempted rape. He was interrogated for a lengthy time and essentially told how he committed the crime (*Fikes v. Alabama*, 1957). In Florida, forty African Americans were arrested for questioning in the murder of a White man. For several defendants, the interrogation began in the afternoon and continued until sunrise. At one point during the night, the state attorney was called and wrote down a confession. At the end, he tore it up and told the interrogators that the confession was unsatisfactory. The state attorney scolded the interrogators and told them not to call him again until they got something better. Three defendants pled guilty and were given the death penalty, and one was convicted and given the death penalty following a jury trial (*Chambers et al. v. Florida*, 1940).

A foundation of the American criminal justice system is that a defendant is tried by his or her peers. However, this has not been the case for African Americans, and when it does exist, it is a very, very recent phenomenon. African Americans have long been tried by all-White juries where the acquittal rate was virtually nonexistent when White individuals were alleged to be the victims. Because African Americans had a more difficult time qualifying to vote, they could not serve on juries. If a few were qualified to serve on juries, White prosecutors were able to keep them off juries.

When the U.S. Supreme Court finally outlawed the poll tax, a measure that kept many African Americans from jury service, a number of states began to color-code prospective jurors (*Avery v. Georgia*, 1953). For instance, in the early 1950s the population of Fulton County (Atlanta), Georgia, was 691,797. Of this total, 525,983 (76%) were White and 165,814 (24%) were African Americans. Only 17,736 African Americans were eligible to serve on juries. An African American male was accused of sexually assaulting a White female. A jury list was drawn up that included 20,509 Whites and 1,115 African Americans. White persons were designated by their names on white slips of paper and African Americans by yellow slips of paper. Since there were several divisions of court, 150 to 200 individuals were chosen for each court division. A judge testified that he drew 60 persons "randomly" and all 60 were White. The African American defendant was convicted and sentenced to die in Georgia's electric chair (*Avery v. Georgia*, 1953). Although the U.S. Supreme Court held the practice of differentiating jurors by colors of paper to be blatant racial discrimination, this practice continued into the late 1960s (*Venable v. A/S Forenede Dampskibsselskab*, 1967).

Moreover, discrimination in jury selection continued into the 1980s. A veteran prosecutor in Philadelphia instructed new prosecutors not to select African Americans as jurors because African Americans were more prone to acquit. The practice of having a few African Americans on juries is a recent phenomenon, having been assured in the late 1980s and 1990s by several U.S. Supreme Court rulings on jury selection (*Batson v. Kentucky*, 1986; *Edmonson v. Leesville Concrete Co.*, 1991; *Powers v. Ohio*, 1991).

Presently, criticism is voiced against predominately African American juries in predominately African American cities and areas, such as the Bronx in New York City, "downtown" Los Angeles, California, and Washington, DC. The charge is that African Americans generally are not pro–law enforcement or prosecution. Shortly after O. J. Simpson was charged with killing his former wife and her friend, discussions emerged whether O. J. Simpson would be tried "downtown" or in Santa Monica. The difference was that the "downtown" juries were more mixed than Santa Monica juries.

In predominately African American cities and communities, African American jurors convict African American defendants regularly. Every defendant who is tried is not necessarily guilty, or may be guilty but guilt has not been established beyond a reasonable doubt, the standard that is used in criminal law. In the latter situations, African Americans are more likely to acquit, unlike predominantly White juries, which have had a history of convicting African Americans on little or no evidence and doing so in record time.

The Relevance of the Past to the Present

Today, one might now argue that court rulings and attitudes from the nineteenth century and early twentieth century are irrelevant to today's society as we enter the twenty-first century. In fact, Whites and some conservative African Americans say that slavery, white supremacy, and Jim Crow laws have nothing to do with present society. But race remains a salient factor. Attitudes from the past are still relevant, operating in present society, and reflective in current policy areas.

For example, Jacobs and Carmichael (2002) studied the reenactment of death penalty laws after the U.S. Supreme Court held in *Furman v. Georgia* (1972) that the manner in which the death penalty had been imposed was cruel and unusual punishment. States were instructed to pass new death penalty statutes. Jacobs and Carmichael found that the degree of economic inequality and the extent of Republican control of state legislatures were important variables in states passing new death penalty statutes. But another important variable emerged as significant, which was the number of African Americans in a state. They found that the more African Americans in a state, the quicker the state created a new death penalty statute (Jacobs & Carmichael, 2002). This finding reflects the type of fear and social control created through the Black Codes that were passed immediately after the end of slavery.

In another link to the past, the U.S. Supreme Court rejected explicit references to African Americans in state statutes for discrimination (Clark, 1973). It held as unconstitutional a law in West Virginia which explicitly said that only White males could serve on juries (*Strauder v. West Virginia*, 1880). It also rejected a Louisiana law that made explicit references to African Americans (Clark, 1973). Although this was good, the Court suggested indirectly that the proper way to discriminate against African Americans was not to refer specifically to them in the Constitution or state statutes like the colorblind Mississippi Constitution. States could ascertain traits, behaviors, and characteristics of African Americans and outlaw these without references to them specifically. As an illustration, most African Americans did not own land and did not have money after leaving slavery. Accordingly, the way to oppress them politically was favoring people who had land, could pay a poll tax, and could read and write, which African Americans were forbidden to do since being in slavery. Current courts are using these same standards today, signaling that as long as a racial distinction is not explicitly made, the courts will uphold current practices. This argument is supported extensively in subsequent chapters.

African Americans have been condemned over the issue of affirmative action, which has been linked to quotas. Conservatives and politicians have charged that quotas are bad for society and incompatible with American principles. These same individuals disregard the fact that Whites have always practiced affirmative action for themselves and utilized quotas—reserving plum jobs for their friends and children and having all Whites and zero African Americans or mostly Whites with a token African American. Whites have been led to believe that many African Americans have jobs and positions that they are not entitled to have and have deprived deserving Whites of employment. These arguments are the basis for attacks on affirmative action today. However, statistics fail to support such a belief, as African Americans have long had a high unemployment rate and are seldom found in top managerial positions. The few affirmative action slots constitute a miniscule number of positions. Still, charges have been leveled that African Americans want quotas, and the response by most Whites is that quotas are anathema to America. But quotas are only bad when race is involved and particularly when African Americans are said to be benefiting. Quotas are not bad when Whites benefit.

As an illustration, the current Congress and the U.S. Supreme Court, under Title IX, have supported quotas for female athletes (Whittaker, 1997). This federal law forbids discrimination in college and high school sports. To avoid discrimination, colleges were mandated to give scholarships on a sixty-forty ratio involving men and women or the proportion of women matriculating at a college (Campbell, 1995). Colleges, to reach this quota, have had to add sports programs for women and/or cut sports for men (Schuld, 1998). At some schools, scholarships must be allocated according to the percentage of females on campus. For instance, Brown's female athletes argued that women constituted 51 percent of the student population at Brown University, but 38 percent of the athletes at Brown were women. This, according to the women athletes, constituted gender discrimination. Both a U.S. district court and the Second Circuit Court of Appeals agreed. The U.S. Supreme Court refused to hear this case, indirectly upholding the lower federal courts (Gavora, 1998).

Interestingly, most of the added sports for women involve sports that benefit White females (Gavora, 1996; Holley, 1995). For instance, Ohio State University operates the largest athletic program in the country, awarding 866 scholarships to both men and women athletes. To increase the number of scholarships given to women, such sports as hockey, soccer, lacrosse, and crew were added. In 1999, Ohio State proposed to add a "light crew" for smaller women. Women's crew involves seventy to one hundred women with recruitment being done from ex-volleyball players, ex-swimmers, and ex-soccer players. A picture of the crew team showed that all members were White females (Powers, 1998). Essentially, what is being done is giving mostly White females free college education.

There have not been strong criticisms from the public, Congress, or opponents of quotas, such as those voiced when quotas are linked to race. Quotas are bad if they are perceived as benefiting African Americans, but they are not bad when mostly White female athletes benefit (Parker, 1998). Undoubtedly, African Americans have been discriminated against in coaching at predominately White universities and colleges. However, if supporters of African American coaches advocated that they hold 60 percent of all coaching jobs with White and other coaches taking the other 40 percent, Whites, Congress, and the courts would loudly condemn this position as a quota that is un-American and illegal.

At many large universities, the money to fund sports comes from football and men's basketball—sports that are dominated by African Americans. It is not unusual to see an all-African American starting five or four-out-of-five starting on basketball teams at many major predominately White universities. Following the 1998 football season and the 1999 bowl games, the number one team in college football had all African Americans starting on defense, and nine or ten members of the starting eleven on offense. Ironically, African American athletes are helping to fund athletic opportunities for White female athletes that are based on a quota requirement. But if African Americans are perceived as benefiting from quotas, there is a loud hue and cry from coast to coast.

Moreover, women fare better than African Americans in the area of affirmative action programs to address discrimination. Early in the women's movement, arguments were advanced that gender discrimination is as pernicious as, and is on a par with, racial discrimination, and this assertion was stated in the case involving Virginia's attempt to bar women from admission to Virginia Military Institute (VMI) (*United States v. Virginia et al.*, 1996). However, the current U.S. Supreme Court has established two standards for establishing discrimination with respect to race and gender. The standard for judging an affirmative action program for African Americans is higher and tougher than that for an affirmative action program for women (Asseo, 1996; Reed, 1996). Moreover, the U.S. Supreme Court has rejected statistical evidence in an employment case involving African Americans (*Wards Cove Packing Co, Inc. v. Atonio et al.*, 1989) and in a case involving capital punishment (*McCleskey v. Kemp*, 1987). The justices on the U.S. Supreme Court are quite hostile when allegations of racial discrimination are argued in cases (Holmes, 1997; "Legal Gerrymandering," 1997; "Settlement May Avert Affirmative Action Test," 1997), but they are sensitive to the arguments regarding gender discrimination (*United States v. Virginia*, 1996). Statistical arguments based on race are rejected, but statistical arguments based on the percentage of women in a college student body are compelling. This current difference in race and sex discrimination cases reflects the same type of differentiation made in the late 1800s involving the Chinese laundries in San Francisco and African Americans in Mississippi.

A final link from the past to the present is shown by an Alabama case involving two African Americans who filed a lawsuit alleging racial discrimination due to changes made in county governments immediately after they were elected. In addition, they stated that the Alabama counties had not precleared their changes with the U.S. Department of Justice as required by the Voting Rights Act of 1965. A majority of the U.S. Supreme Court expressed concern with the rights of the state. Justice Anthony Kennedy declared that if federalism is to function as a practical system of governance, states must be allowed predictability and efficiency in structuring their governments. Three justices dissented and charged that the majority ignored the intent and purpose of the Voting Rights Act of 1965. Congress enacted it as a response to the *unremitting and ingenious defiance of the Fifteenth Amendment for nearly a century by state officials* in certain parts of this country. In short, counties have innumerable ways to disenfranchise African Americans and dilute their voting. The majority, however, was unconcerned about this historical fact and chose to sympathize with state governments (*Presley v. Etowah County Commissioner et al.*, 1992). The counties should have been asked to explain why the changes in critical policies occurred just after African Americans won elections that have always been dominated by Whites. Justice Kennedy's voicing concerns for state governments is similar to the expression of concerns and sympathy for Whites after Reconstruction and during the reign of white supremacy.

Conclusion

An editorial in the *Detroit News* reflected on the legacy of *Plessy v. Ferguson* upon its one hundredth anniversary. This editorial noted that the rationale used to decide *Plessy* is still with the American people today. Then, the Court held that the Fourteenth Amendment did not outlaw racial classification, holding that the government could not engage in arbitrary and unreasonable racial distinction. In *Plessy*, the separate-but-equal doctrine was held to be reasonable. Later, in *Brown v. Board of Education*, the racial classification was held to be unreasonable because it was damaging to African American children. In *Bakke*, the first case to test affirmative action, the racial classification was held to be unreasonable. Although the lone dissenter in *Plessy*, Justice Harlan, stated that the Constitution is colorblind, the U.S. Supreme Court has never held that the Constitution is colorblind. Instead, any racial classification must be judged based on whether the government or state has been reasonable in its classification ("The Legacy of Plessy," 1996).

Just as the legal test for deciding racial classification still exists today, other features and attitudes of that era still exist. For instance, in 1890, Mississippi sought to oppress and discriminate against African Americans by excluding them from the political process and thereby assuring their powerlessness. Restrained by the Fourteenth Amendment, the State of Mississippi could not write its Constitution to ensure white supremacy with references to race in it. As a result, on the surface, African Americans were never mentioned for discrimination and oppression. Mississippians pretended that they were being "colorblind," and the U.S. Supreme Court upheld the Mississippi strategy in 1898. A hundred years later in 1998, the U.S. Supreme Court has endorsed a similar strategy, like its brother justices in 1898. Hence, a law punishing African Americans more harshly for using crack cocaine than Whites who use powder cocaine is legal although the drugs are the same. Similarly, a law that executed only African Americans for allegedly raping White females was legal. When these laws were challenged, the Court looked at the statute and concluded that race was not mentioned in the statute. Thus, they were legal regardless of what the statistical evidence showed.

Yet, statistical evidence has been viewed differently depending upon who has been affected. This means African Americans receive one type of justice and others receive a different type of justice. As an illustration, in the case involving the Chinese laundries in 1886, the U.S. Supreme Court noted that those individuals arrested under San Francisco were all Chinese except for one White individual. This ordinance was held to be unconstitutional, but discrimination against African Americans ten years later was constitutional. This differential treatment suggests the following hypothesis. A dispute between Suburb A and Suburb B likely will be decided using one legal test; however, a dispute between Suburb A and Inner City C will be decided by a much higher and tougher legal test when Inner City C is complaining of unfair treatment.

Although African Americans were freed by President Abraham Lincoln's proclamation, significant discrimination and oppression existed until the 1960s. It was not until the early 1960s that the U.S. Supreme Court ruled as unconstitutional the last of the laws from the Jim Crow era. The freedom that African Americans have is relatively new—*about forty years or less*. This degree of freedom is unlike the freedom afforded to Irish Americans, Jewish Americans, Italian Americans, and even Asian Americans. There is no *Dred Scott v. Sandford* or *Plessy v. Ferguson* for these other ethnic groups. African Americans have always had a unique position among ethnic groups. Even Native Americans, according to Justice Curtis in the Dred Scott case, could become U.S. citizens, provided Native Americans chose to leave the reservations and abandon their "savage" ways. Comparing the status of African Americans and Chinese, Justice Harlan in *Plessy* stated that Whites were perturbed by the Chinese and did not want them to become citizens, but the Chinese could sit with Whites on a train in Louisiana. As one fair-minded U.S. Supreme Court justice pondered, why was it that Whites, who enjoyed greater numbers in the population, and more wealth, political acumen, and social status than African Americans, were so concerned and preoccupied with their need to oppress and discriminate? Whites' needs and fears make justice more difficult for African Americans to achieve. The remaining chapters elaborate upon these injustices.

2

African Americans and Higher Education

Rudolph Alexander Jr. and Mattie Grooms

EDUCATIONAL CONFLICTS HAVE always swirled around African Americans (Bond, 1934; Bullock, 1967). As slaves, African Americans were taught only enough to speak and understand basic English. The slave shacks were color-coded so those slaves would not need to learn how to read signs. Under pains of punishment, they were forbidden to learn how to read and write. Following slavery, acquiring education was problematic. The Ku Klux Klan physically attacked African Americans in some areas simply for trying to learn how to read and write. Moreover, African Americans did not control the expenditures to educate themselves or their children. If a college sought to accept African Americans, segregation laws prevented such colleges, under the pain of a criminal conviction, from educating African Americans near White students (*Berea College v. Kentucky*, 1908). In the South, African Americans were not accepted at major White universities until the 1960s, and then it was done reluctantly and in an atmosphere of violence.

As the millennium begins, a survey of the educational landscape reveals that there are still issues involving African Americans. Contention and strife are occurring over admissions to universities and race-based scholarships, as some universities try to increase the admission of African American students and retain them (Platt, 1997). This current issue revolves around affirmative action and quotas.

While Whites have always utilized quotas in many areas (i.e., 100 percent Whites and 0 percent African Americans or one token African American), quotas have only recently been anathematized. Quotas have been linked to affirmative action, a policy developed during President John F. Kennedy's administration in the early 1960s. Currently, affirmative action is viewed synonymously with quotas, suggesting to many persons that less qualified African Americans are receiving educational opportunities that should go to Whites (Lewis & Patram, 1998; Turner, 1998). While women and Hispanics have benefited from affirmative action, affirmative action is now colored with a black face. For instance, an African American who was at the medical school during the Bakke case experienced some legal problems, which were quickly blamed by conservatives as being the fault of affirmative action (Marquis, 1998). Like the picture of welfare, affirmative action has a black face, which incurs attacks, criticisms, and hostilities.

This chapter focuses upon issues of race in higher education. First, it reviews the historical background involving education and African Americans. Second, it discusses the issue of race and law in keeping African Americans from White universities. Third, it discusses the development of affirmative action and its relevance to higher education. Fourth, it reviews the issue of race and law involving White persons who were denied admission to professional programs. Fifth, it critiques the critics of affirmative action in higher education.

Historical Review

In 1862, Congress passed the Morrill Land Grant Act, which provided states with land to establish colleges for citizens. Essentially, these newly established colleges were for White citizens. In 1890, Congress passed a second Morrill Land Grant Act essentially for African Americans, creating sixteen colleges, most of which were in the South (Wilson, 1994).

Negatively affecting education as well as other social life was the U.S. Supreme Court decision in *Plessy v. Ferguson* (1896). From the outset, *Plessy* allowed states to adopt educational policies that blatantly discriminated against African Americans (Darboe, 2003). Prior to the court ruling in *Plessy*, segregation was an American way of life, a fact first acknowledged in national policy by the Morrill Act of 1890. That statute required states with dual systems of education to divide their federal land-grant funds between White and Black institutions on an equitable [*sic*] basis (Holmes, 1969). The importance of the *Plessy* decision to public and higher education stems not only from its precedent that mandated the practice of separate-but-equal, but also from the latitude the case had given to the concept of equality under the veil of states' rights. *Plessy* accepted a legal definition of race that was already being employed by states to allocate public and private benefits and privileges prejudicially, and it upheld state autonomy in educational policymaking.

Race, Admission, and the Courts: Keeping African Americans Out, Part I

One of the early cases involving race and admission in higher education involved Lloyd Gaines in 1936. Gaines, an African American and graduate of Lincoln University, sought a legal education. Lincoln University, an all-African American university in Missouri, did not have a law school, and so Gaines applied to the University of Missouri Law School. Gaines was denied admittance to the University of Missouri Law School, although it acknowledged that his work and credits qualified him for admission. Then, the laws of Missouri required separation of African American and White students. Gaines sought to compel his admission in the Missouri courts, but these efforts were fruitless. Consequently, he appealed to the U.S. Supreme Court, and the Court found that he was entitled to legal training, but not necessarily at the University of Missouri (*Missouri ex rel. Gaines v. Canada*, 1938).

The Missouri legislature had authorized the curators of Lincoln University to provide education training comparable to Whites in Missouri. If an African American wanted a legal education, the curators at Lincoln University were obligated to pay out-of-state tuition in one of several adjacent states (i.e., Kansas, Nebraska, Iowa, or Illinois) that admitted African Americans. The Court held that Gaines had harmed his case by not requesting a legal education from the curators of Lincoln University (*Missouri ex rel. Gaines v. Canada*, 1938).

The Court did hold that the State of Missouri erred in not establishing a law school for African Americans. According to the justices, the Fourteenth Amendment to the U.S. Constitution and the equal protection clause required *a pledge of the protection of equal laws*. This interpretation means that a state had to enact equal laws, and the failure of Missouri to provide separate but equal legal training violated the Fourteenth Amendment. The Court stressed that Missouri, and any other state, was entitled to considerable latitude in judging the comparability of separate facilities for Whites and African Americans, and the federal courts should not second-guess the equality of opportunities (*Missouri ex rel. Gaines v. Canada*, 1938).

In another case, the U.S. Supreme Court ordered the admittance of Ada Lois Sipuel, an African American female, to the law school of the University of Oklahoma, where the only law school in the state was located (*Sipuel v. Board of Regents of the University of Oklahoma*, 1948). However, it sanctioned Oklahoma's strategy to obstruct her admission (*Fisher v. Hurst*, 1948). Sipuel was considered to be qualified to be admitted to the University of Oklahoma Law School and was rejected solely based on her color. She was unsuccessful in convincing the Oklahoma courts to force her admittance. The Court held that Sipuel could not be denied admittance and remanded the case to the

Oklahoma courts for further proceedings, which was consistent with the Court's opinion (*Sipuel v. Board of Regents of the University of Oklahoma*, 1948). On remand, the Oklahoma court directed the Oklahoma Board of Regents to enroll Sipuel in the first-year class at the University of Oklahoma Law School, until a separate school was created for African Americans, or not enroll any student in the University of Oklahoma first-year class until a separate school was established and ready to open (*Fisher v. Hurst*, 1948). Despite that obvious intent to avoid Sipuel's admittance, the U.S. Supreme Court ruled that the Oklahoma court's action was consistent with its opinion (*Fisher v. Hurst*, 1948).

In 1950, the U.S. Supreme Court seemed to be close to changing its acceptance of separate but equal in a Texas case. Perhaps sensing the critical nature of this case, a number of southern states, through their attorneys general, urged the U.S. Supreme Court to uphold the principle pronounced in *Plessy v. Ferguson* (1896). These states were Arkansas, Florida, Georgia, Kentucky, Louisiana, Mississippi, North Carolina, Oklahoma, South Carolina, Tennessee, and Virginia. The Texas case involved Herman Sweatt, who sought admission to the University of Texas Law School, which was the only law school in Texas.

A lower Texas court case agreed that Sweatt's rights under the Fourteenth Amendment had been violated by his rejection to the University of Texas Law School located in Austin, Texas. However, this court refused to order his admittance. Instead, the court put off a remedy for six months, giving the state of Texas time to create a law school for African Americans. The state of Texas quickly created a makeshift law school in Houston, Texas, that was called the Texas State University (now Texas Southern University). The faculty consisted of four temporary members of the University of Texas Law School in Austin. The library at the newly established law school for African Americans was quite limited, but the state of Texas stated that students could use library resources at the State Law Library in the Capital Building, which was in Austin, Texas, and was 186 miles from Houston. Accepting these quick changes, the Texas courts ruled that the state had created equal facilities for African Americans and Sweatt's case was dismissed. Upon appeal to the U.S. Supreme Court, the Court ruled that the law school created in Houston, Texas, was not equal to the University of Texas Law School and ordered that Sweatt be admitted (*Sweatt v. Painter et al.*, 1950). *Sweatt* was the first case in which the U.S. Supreme Court was willing to second-guess a state about the equality of opportunity provided to African Americans.

As stated, this case was believed by some to be critical and some persons felt that the Court might overturn *Plessy*. However, the Court declined to go further than the issues in the case. The Court reminded interested parties that "broader issues have been urged for our consideration, but we adhere to the principle of deciding constitutional questions only in the context of the particular case before the Court" (*Sweatt v. Painter et al.*, 1950, p. 631).

Interestingly, the U.S. Supreme Court seemed to endorse the principle of diversity in *Sweatt*. Writing for the majority, Justice Fred Vinson wrote:

> Although the law is a highly learned profession, we are well aware that it is an intensely practical one. The law school, the proving ground for legal learning and practice, cannot be effective in isolation from the individuals and institutions with which the law interacts. Few students and no one who has practiced law would choose to study in an academic vacuum, removed from the interplay of ideas and the exchange of views with which the law is concerned. The law school to which Texas is willing to admit petitioner excludes from its student body members of the racial groups which number 85 percent of the population of the State and include most of the lawyers, witnesses, jurors, judges and other officials with whom petitioner will inevitably be dealing when he becomes a member of the Texas Bar. With such a substantial and significant segment of society excluded, we cannot conclude that the education offered petitioner is substantially equal to that which he would receive if admitted to the University of Texas Law School. (*Sweatt v. Painter et al.*, 1950, p. 634)

In the 1960s, a few African American students were admitted to universities in the south, but it was done in a highly publicized atmosphere of hatred and violence. Most noticeably, these enrollments occurred at the University of Georgia, the University of Mississippi, and the University of Alabama. At all three universities, federal troops had to be called to protect these students from violence. Because these students were not wanted and were not wanted at other institutions, the enrollment of African Americans at White universities was always very small.

The Creation of Affirmative Action

Although affirmative action is associated with race, its roots lie within the struggle during the 1930s over social insurance, public assistance, and entitlement programs (Platt, 1997). For instance, the 1935 Wagner Act gave the National Labor Relations Board the power to rectify unjust conditions in the labor industry (Platt, 1997). Later in 1941, President Roosevelt, by executive order, decreed that military contractors could not discriminate against minorities in employment (Garcia, 1997).

Affirmative action was first linked to civil rights by President Kennedy's executive order in 1961 (Livington, 1996; Platt, 1997), and President Kennedy was the first person to use officially the term "affirmative action" (Garcia, 1997). It instructed contractors doing business with the federal government to hire African Americans and women in their businesses. Failure to do so could incur the loss of federal contracts. The Office of Federal Contract Compliance was created to monitor adherence (Simmons, 1982). Later, Title VI of the Civil Rights Act of 1964 authorized quotas and preferential hiring when past discrimination had been established against minorities and women.

Affirmative action had come to be defined as a compilation of laws, policies, guidelines, and administrative practices geared toward ending discrimination against persons perceived to be different or inferior (Bond, 1998; Francis, 1993). Its primary aim was to reduce present discrimination and increase the presence of minorities and women in universities and colleges (Feinberg, 1998). Because African Americans and women had been excluded from society by intentional and institutional racism and sexism, eliminating discrimination only was insufficient. Affirmative steps were needed to overcome institutional and cultural barriers in order for these excluded groups to gain entrance to the mainstream of society. As a critical aspect of entrance and advancement, colleges and universities needed to be receptive to and practice affirmative action (Howard, 1997). Colleges and universities were viewed as the key environments to produce long-lasting effects.

Early on, the term affirmative action was quickly linked with preferential treatment and quotas for African Americans (Beauchamp, 1993; Howard, 1997). Also, some persons began to voice sentiments of unfairness (Arneson, 1993; Oldenquist, 1993; Rachels, 1993, Wolf-Devine, 1993). Seats in colleges and universities are highly valued and limited commodities (Cahn, 1993). For instance, a medical or legal career can lead to a very high standard of living, and thus being admitted to medical school or law school is a prize that can produce conflict for those not admitted (Slocum, 1993). Even admittance to colleges and universities to pursue degrees in other professions, such as journalism or social work, or a social science degree, along with the awarding of scholarships, can provoke some conflict (Kauffman & Gonzalez, 1997).

Race, Admission, and the Courts: Discriminating against Whites or Keeping African Americans Out, Part II

Nearly twenty-five years after *Sweatt*, the U.S. Supreme Court heard a case involving a White male who contended that he was illegally denied admission to the University of Washington Law School. The case began in a state court in Washington. There, Marco DeFunis, the White male involved, argued that the school operated an illegal admission policy. The law school had spaces for 150 students and normally accepted about 275, with an expected attrition of 125 students. About 1601 applicants applied for the slots. African Americans, American Indians, Filipinos, and Hispanics were reviewed differently from White applicants in that they were not summarily rejected for failing to achieve a minimum score and were reviewed by a special committee. Thirty-six of thirty-seven minorities admitted to the University of Washington Law School had scores lower than DeFunis. In addition, forty-eight nonminorities were admitted who also had scores lower than DeFunis and twenty-three of them were veterans.

The lower Washington court held that this admission strategy was illegal and ordered that DeFunis be admitted. The Supreme Court of Washington held that the admission procedure was not discriminatory. One U.S. Supreme Court Justice stayed the decision of the Supreme Court of Washington until the entire U.S. Supreme Court had ruled, which permitted DeFunis to continue school. When the case finally reached the U.S. Supreme Court docket, the issue of mootness came up because DeFunis was very close to finishing law school. At oral arguments, DeFunis was in his last term of law school. Realizing that DeFunis would be finished with law school by the time a decision was rendered, the Court vacated the decision of the Supreme Court of Washington and remanded the case because of mootness (*DeFunis et al. v. Odegaard et al.*, 1974). In other words, the Court never decided the merit of the case. However, U.S. Supreme Court Justice William Douglas did not agree with the majority that the case was moot, conveying in his dissenting opinion that DeFunis' case had merit and that he had been illegally discriminated against by officials of the law school (*DeFunis et al. v. Odegaard et al.*, 1974).

Although the U.S. Supreme Court did not decide the merits of the DeFunis case, Justice Douglas stated that it should have been decided because it involved a serious national issue. Supporting Justice Douglas' view were the number of organizations that filed amici curiae (i.e., friend of the court) briefs. Among the groups supporting the legal views of DeFunis were the Chamber of Commerce of the United States; American Federation of Labor, Congress of Industrial Organizations; American Jewish Congress; Jewish Rights Council; Advocate Society; and Anti-Defamation League of B'nai B'rith. Urging the Court to rule against DeFunis were the State of Ohio; the City of Seattle; American Bar Association; President and Fellows of Harvard College; Center for Law and Education at Harvard University; Board of Governors of Rutgers, State University of New Jersey; Deans of the Antioch School of Law; Association of American Law Schools; Association of American Medical Colleges; a group of law school deans; Law School Admission Council; Mexican American Legal Defense and Educational Fund; Council on Legal Education Opportunity; Lawyers' Committee for Civil Rights Under Law;

NAACP Legal Defense and Educational Fund; National Conference of Black Lawyers; American Indian Law Students Association; Legal Aid Society of Alameda County; National Organization for Women Legal Defense and Education Fund; and the National Council of Jewish Women (*DeFunis et al. v. Odegaard et al.*, 1974).

A few years later, the U.S. Supreme Court heard the case of Alan Bakke, who was denied admission to the medical school at the University of California at Davis. The school had slots for 100 students and designated sixteen slots for disadvantaged minorities. Similar to the law school at the University of Washington, a special admission committee considered all the minority applicants, while a regular committee considered the White applicants. Bakke contended that he was discriminated against because minorities with lower scores were admitted. In a very split decision, a majority of the Justices held that the admission policy violated the Fourteenth Amendment to the U.S. Constitution. Justice Lewis Powell, writing for the majority, stated that the medical school could not provide a satisfactory legal justification for its policy. Justice Powell further noted that an admission committee might consider race as one factor in its admission decisions. According to Justice Powell, the model used at Harvard University was legal because it strove to achieve a diverse student body, believing it was critical to students getting a broad education. While all students must be qualified to enter Harvard, among this group of qualified students are applicants from farm areas, applicants from the West Coast, applicants from the South, and applicants from other countries. In addition, Harvard wants women, urbanites, rural persons, and minorities. There is no limit on the number of each group to be admitted. Justice Powell stated that if the University of California at Davis had followed the Harvard model, the policy would be constitutional (*Regents of the University of California v. Bakke*, 1978).

In 1996, the Fifth Circuit Court of Appeals, however, mounted a serious assault on affirmative action in education and stated that race may not be a factor in any admission decision. This occurred in a case involving White applicants who failed to get into the University of Texas law school. Four law school students sued because they had been rejected for admission, contending that less qualified African Americans and Hispanics were given special consideration during an affirmative action program.

The law school received over four thousand applicants for a class of five hundred. To reach this admission target, the law school admitted about nine hundred, knowing that about four hundred would not come or would attend other schools. Because of the sheer number of applications, administrative staffs were authorized to admit presumptively some applicants and reject presumptively some applicants. Panels of law professors would review applicants in the midrange. Because the University of Texas historically had had low minority enrollment, a special panel reviewed almost all of them, and some of them were admitted with scores slightly lower than the four White applicants who sued. They won their case in a trial before a U.S. district court judge; however, this judge ruled that, while the admission was flawed, race could be constitutionally used in the admission process. However, on appeal, the Fifth Circuit Court of Appeals strongly rejected that race could be used at all in an admission process (*Hopwood v. State of Texas*, 1996).

In the Bakke case, which involved admission to a medical school, the U.S. Supreme Court in a split five-to-four decision held that an illegal quota had been used to deny admission to Bakke. A member of the majority, Justice Powell, held that race could be used as one of many factors in admission decisions. But according to the judges on the Fifth Circuit Court of Appeals, no other U.S. Supreme Court Justice joined that conclusion. Accordingly, in the opinion of the Fifth Circuit Court, the view that race could be one of many factors in admission decisions represented one Justice's view, and one U.S. Supreme Court Justice cannot establish constitutional law. For this reason, the Fifth Circuit Court was free to reject Bakke, and, looking at other U.S. Supreme Court decisions involving affirmative action in other areas, the Fifth Circuit Court of Appeals held that race cannot be a factor in admission decisions (*Hopwood v. State of Texas*, 1996).

More important, an increasing number of courts have ruled as the Fifth Circuit Court had in Hopwood and held that race cannot be a factor in college and university admission decisions (*Honadle v. University of Vermont & State Agri College*, 1999; *Keeley Tatsuyo Hunter v. The Regents of the University of California*, 1999; *Smith v. The University of Washington Law School*, 1998; *Wooden v. Board of Regents of the Univ. Sys. of Georgia*, 1999).

A Critique of the Critics of Affirmative Action in Education

Conservative views held by law professors, think tanks, and judges declare that society should be colorblind, as U.S. Supreme Court Justice John Harlan urged in *Plessy* in 1896. They say also that the U.S. Constitution is colorblind and thus race cannot or should not be a factor in any educational decision. Had these individuals been alive during *Plessy*, it is very doubtful that they would have supported Justice Harlan in *Plessy*. While on the surface these views seem grand, they insidiously reflect the same views and objectives of the virulent white supremacists of the nineteenth and early twentieth centuries.

The Fifth Circuit Court panel that decided *Hopwood* voiced sentiments and philosophies consistent with the white supremacists of the late nineteenth century or one hundred years ago. As an illustration, Circuit Court Judge Jerry E. Smith in the *Hopwood* case wrote the following:

> While the use of race per se is proscribed, state-supported schools may reasonably consider a host of factors—some of which may have some correlation with race—in making admissions decisions. The federal courts have no warrant to intrude on those executive and legislative judgments unless the distinctions intrude on specific provisions of federal law or the Constitution. A university may properly favor one applicant over another because of his ability to play the cello, make a downfield tackle, or understand chaos theory. An admission process may also consider an applicant's home state or relationship to school alumni. Law schools specifically may look at things such as unusual or substantial extracurricular activities in college, which may be atypical factors affecting undergraduate grades. Schools may even consider factors such as whether an applicant's parents attended college or the applicant's economic and social background. (*Hopwood v. State of Texas*, 1996, p. 946)

While Circuit Court Judge Smith was laying out reportedly constitutional ways of making admission decisions, he was also laying out ways to discriminate against some applicants. This is no different than what white supremacists had done in Mississippi during the late nineteenth century and that a number of other states modeled. For instance, Mississippi sought to disenfranchise African Americans; however, the officials could not openly state this aim. Thus, knowing that no slaves have ever voted, Mississippi passed a law that if one's grandfather did not vote, one could not vote. Few African Americans could read and write; therefore, literacy became a criterion for voting. Following Mississippi's lead, Alabama studied the type of crimes for which African Americans went to court and made these crimes disqualifying. Further, it added moral turpitude, which was thought to apply to all African Americans, who were considered immoral and amoral people.

Judge Smith's blueprint can have nefarious objectives, although race is not used. For instance, having a criterion that an applicant can receive favoritism because his or her parents went to college benefits Whites. A number of factors correlate with race, as Judge Smith intimated. Voting, home ownership, participation in the stock market, computer ownership, and membership in country clubs are associated with race, economics, and social background. According to Judge Smith, a law school can favor an applicant who plays the cello. If that is true, then it can favor applicants who play golf and tennis, activities that Whites engage in significantly more often than African Americans. Using several of these "race-neutral" factors can eliminate most African Americans from colleges and universities, just as the white supremacists eliminated the vote from African Americans.

Despite what Judge Smith wrote, his views and opinions would be different if Whites were disadvantaged. For instance, a number of mostly African American colleges are becoming increasingly White (Cobbs, 1991). White students, who years ago would not attend a predominately black college, are now attending these schools to the point that Whites make up a majority. For instance, Lincoln University, founded in 1866 by African American Union veterans, in 1989 had a 70 percent White student body and a faculty that was 78 percent non-African American (Sawyers, 1989). Suppose a group of African American administrators, concerned about the increasing number of White students at their schools, sought to reverse this trend and rid their institutions of White students.

To carry out this plan to eliminate White admissions, the school might adopt a race-neutral admission policy that purposely favors African American applicants. Hence, the criteria for admission would include such factors as whether an applicant likes rhythm and blues music, whether an applicant played basketball or had relatives who played basketball, whether an applicant lived in a zip code area or adjacent to a zip code area that had a high crime rate, and whether an applicant lived in an zip code area or adjacent to a zip code area that had a high poverty rate. Additional criteria would be whether an applicant had a family history of diabetes, high blood pressure, or sickle cell anemia. Furthermore, an applicant with a family member in prison, on parole, or probation would be preferred. The last criterion would be that applicants would race. Those applicants who ran the fastest for fifty yards would be preferred. With these criteria in place, a school could rid its university of all White students.

The question, then, is raised as to whether Judge Smith and the other judges on the Fifth Circuit Court of Appeals would sanction such a race-neutral strategy. The author would suggest that these judges would find such an admission plan flawed, if it were implemented at Texas Southern University, a predominately African American higher education institution within the jurisdiction of the Fifth Circuit. If 70 percent of the students at Texas Southern University were White and a new admission strategy reduced subsequent admissions of White students to 0 percent, these judges would find these criteria legally flawed.

An interesting current development, but not an unexpected scenario, is occurring over admissions to universities and colleges in Texas. Texas' use of race in admission decisions was held to be unconstitutional by the Fifth Circuit Court of Appeals, which conservatives in Texas hailed as a just and right decision. Race in admission decisions is illegal and backward, the justices said. As a result, the Texas legislature came up with a race-neutral policy that said that students in the top 10 percent of their class would qualify for admission and race would not be a factor.

Now, the presidents of the two flagship universities in Texas—the University of Texas and Texas A & M—the governor of Texas, several state senators, and numerous parents are opposed to the 10 percent plan (Glater, 2004). Their criticism now is that students in competitive schools, which is their code word for White, are being denied admission because too many students from the less competitive inner cities, which is their code word for African Americans and Latinos, are getting into the top universities in Texas. The discussions center on school type, which is a proxy for social class (Glater, 2004), which then is a second proxy for race. A movement has developed to change the 10 percent policy in the next term of the Texas legislature in 2005. The new proposal calls for a cap on the number of students from low income schools at 50 percent (D. Springer, Associate Dean for Academic Affairs, School of Social Work, personal communication, November 1, 2004). However, a cap at 50 percent or any percent sounds very much like a quota for White students. If a change in the 10 percent policy occurs, race is not likely to be used but no doubt the aim would be to increase the number of White students from the high social class getting into the University of Texas and Texas A & M.

An interesting side note regarding the discussion of the unfairness of the 10 percent rule to students in demanding high schools is that the University of Texas reported that according to preliminary data, it was likely to get a student body that was more diverse than when the Fifth Circuit Court of Appeals ruled against the University of Texas Law School. The data showed that 6,341 students submitted deposits. Of this total, 298 were African American, 1,146 were Latino, 1,128 were Asian, 23 were Native American, 210 were classified as other, and 3,536 were Anglo or White (Glater, 2004). Thus, African Americans were about 5 percent of applicants, and this percentage was said to be reflective of a more diverse student body than before the outcry over the use of race in the law school that prompted the decision by the Fifth Circuit Court of Appeals.

Lack of Focus on Affirmative Action for Whites

As suggested, Whites have always used quotas and affirmative action for themselves. In passage of the Servicemen's Readjustment Act of 1944 on June 22, 1944 (i.e., the G.I. Bill), Congress enabled over two million servicemen to receive a college education. At that time, a college education was reserved mostly for children of the wealthy, and the common person could not afford a college education. The G.I. Bill provided $500 annually for tuition, free textbooks, and a monthly stipend for living expenses. The program produced dramatic results, especially in the State of Minnesota. A few years before the passage of the G.I. Bill, the University of Minnesota had an enrollment of 14,986 students. But two years after the creation of the G.I. Bill, the enrollment was 27,103. While some of this increase was attributed to an increase in general enrollment, the overwhelming causal factor was the G.I. Bill. Classes were swollen with servicemen, causing some students to sit on the floors and providing opportunities for professors and general students to learn about the horrors of war (Sandvik, 1999).

Most of these servicemen parlayed their affirmative action into good jobs, providing their children a higher standard of living and a college education. Although statistics are difficult to obtain (John Butler, personal communication, May 19, 1999), probably none of the servicemen at the University of Minnesota were African Americans. For sure, no southern White university and few of the bordering states permitted African Americans on their campuses as students at the end of World War II.

Critics of affirmative action decried that Whites, who allegedly were more qualified students, were denied admission to the University of Washington Law School, the University of California at Davis Medical School, and the University of Texas Law School. The basis of this reverse discrimination charge is that the White students had higher grade point averages (GPAs) and Law School Admissions Test (LSAT) scores. These White students had GPAs in the 3.5-to-3.6 range, compared to some African American students with GPAs in the range of 3.1 or 3.2. Yet, no one has provided any research that shows that a student with a higher GPA becomes a more ethical or skilled lawyer than a student with a lower GPA. Similarly, no one has offered research that a student with a GPA that is .5 or .6 higher than another student makes a better medical doctor. While we do not know the college GPA of some lawyers, what difference does it make if Johnny Cochran's college GPA was .3 lower than Robert Shapiro's prior to their going to law school? Both Johnny Cochran and Robert Shapiro are skilled, successful attorneys, and both contributed to the successful defense of O. J. Simpson. If one seat were left in a law school class, why should that seat go to Shapiro? Whites would say that the seat should go to Shapiro if he has a higher GPA and higher LSAT scores, which are indicators of the best qualified.

However, the reason for the emphasis on higher scores is that Whites tend to have higher scores. If Whites did not score higher, then the best-qualified students would be those who exhibit other characteristics that correlate with being White, and these characteristics would be indicators of the best qualified. For instance, the U.S. Department of Education found discrimination against Asians in favor of Whites in admission to a graduate mathematics department. No one charged that the Asians were less qualified because they scored lower than Whites. In fact, the Asians scored higher. The Department of Mathematics found other reasons to find Whites more deserving of admission (Mathews, 1990).

Another flaw in the critics' argument is that they do not look for favoritism in favor of Whites. Every White person who goes to college is not the best qualified. President George W. Bush addressed minority journalists on the subject of legacies in admission and he claimed to be opposed to legacies. Legacy is the practice of giving preference in admission to the offspring of alumni. President Bush's grandfather graduated from Yale, which gave preference to President Bush's father in his admission to Yale (Goldstein, 2004). Because his grandfather and father were alumni, George W. Bush was admitted to Yale. Then, due to these legacies, one of President Bush's daughters was admitted to Yale. However, President Bush said that he is opposed to legacies. Legacies are simply affirmative action for Whites and they favor Whites who have long had access to higher education. Merit does not enter into these discussions and in all probability President Bush was not among the most qualified applicants when he applied to Yale University.

Some White students are average students, and White privilege provides them with opportunities not available to others. For instance, in the DeFunis case, some White students were admitted to the University of Washington Law School and their GPAs were lower than DeFunis. Yet these White students were not challenged for taking a seat that should have gone to DeFunis. While some of these students were likely White veterans, some were not. Simply, these nonveteran White students benefited from White privilege. Perhaps their parents were alumni, or they were related to trustees of the university or had relatives who had given a large sum of money to the law school.

Supporting the above argument, Deborah Brandt (1998/1999), a faculty member at the University of Wisconsin, stated that 27 African American students were admitted to the university with below-average scores of between 16 and 20 on the ACT. However, a White student with a score of 10 was admitted and 5 other White students were admitted with ACT scores of below 16. Admitted also were 429 White students with scores on the ACT between 16 and 20 (Brandt, 1998/1999). Yet, the spotlight is put on 27 African Americans for their allegedly low scores while ignoring the lower scores of Whites and the 429 White students with similar scores.

Some White students are very talented academically and score high on tests and write very well. However, not every White student is brilliant academically. Many are average and below-average students. Brandt (1998/1999) states that "while black students at my university, for instance, may have average scores five points below those of White students on the ACT, this is an aggregate and only proportional statistic. Numerically, there are many more low-scoring White students than low-scoring minority students occupying seats in university classrooms, even though White students' skin color exempts them from stigma. And if you look at the actual test scores of individuals, you will see that most minority students score in the same middling range of standardized tests as most of their White counterparts. The higher overall average among Whites is inflated, in fact, by the presence of students whose parents and grandparents enjoyed access to the university when standards—and tuition—were much lower than they are now" (p. 127).

Another illustration of the lack of focus on quotas and reverse discrimination in education that favors Whites involves athletic programs for women in college and universities. Though quotas are said to be un-American and they are quickly condemned if linked to race, there is virtually no condemnation of the quotas in education for women athletics. Jessica Gavora (1996) stated that Title IX that outlawed sex discrimination had evolved into a quota system that constituted reverse discrimination and was harmful to men and minorities. No conservative group has been clamoring to provide lawyers to fight this reverse discrimination and quota system, as they have for the University of Texas White law students.

At some colleges, African American athletes in nonmajor sports have been victimized in order to create a statistical balance between the male and female proportions on college campuses. When African Americans argue that they should get a specific percentage of scholarships or jobs, this suggestion is quickly and loudly criticized. Yet, women have been permitted a certain percentage of college scholarships based on their proportion on a campus. In order to create these gender percentages, women's basketball teams are allowed two more scholarship players than men, although only five players can play at a time. The sole reason for allowing two more female basketball players is for statistical reasons. At Northern Arizona University, men's swimming and diving were dropped solely to create a majority of scholarships going to women. Women constituted 56 percent of the enrollment. Thus, by dropping men's swimming and diving, the percentage of women receiving college scholarships rose to 51 percent ("College Dropping Swimming, Diving," 1999).

Imagine African Americans constituting 30 percent of the population of a city and demanding 30 percent of the jobs in city hall. Upon finding that African Americans constitute 29 percent of the employees, a decision is made to lay off some Whites so that the percentage for African Americans would rise to 30 percent. Groups would vigorously condemn such a process, and the courts would quickly hold it illegal.

Conclusion

African Americans continue to have a difficult time in higher education. First, they were denied entrance to many colleges and universities for a number of years. Now, their admission has been challenged under the guise that Whites are being discriminated against by affirmative action. The proportion of African Americans who have benefited from affirmative action policies in education is small and pales in comparison to the affirmative action for Whites. In the Bakke case, 16 seats were reserved for minorities, but only a few of these seats went to African Americans. Most went to Asian students. Diminished by high dropout rates for high school students and poverty, the pool of African Americans available to go to higher education is small. These small numbers do not justify the hostility of conservative Whites and the organizations that feel that they must fight "reverse discrimination." If these groups were genuinely standing on principle in their opposition to quotas and affirmative action, then they would single out White females in universities who have athletic quotas and the many Whites in college who have had affirmative action based on White privilege.

3

African American Juveniles and the Justice System

A NUMBER OF LAYPERSONS AND politicians have repeatedly stated that juveniles who commit crimes need to be held responsible for their criminal behaviors (Marx, 1998; Pan, 1998; Wolf, 1999). Further, they state that society needs to get tough on juveniles (Ingram, 1997; Peterson, 1998; Shepardson, 1997; Strausberg, 1998; Suro, 1997; Walston, 1997; Wolf, 1999). The implication of these statements is that juveniles are not held responsible for their offenses and instead are "slapped on the wrist." As a result, each year a state legislature passes legislation designed to get tough on juveniles. The result of the public outcry is that there has been an increased number of juveniles processed and incarcerated by the justice system (Miller, 1996).

Jerome Miller (1996) attributes the change in juveniles' handling to politics and conservative think tanks that have manipulated a crime agenda that has strong racial overtones. In 1964, Barry Goldwater, who was the Republican candidate for president, used crime as a political issue that had racial overtones. In one speech, Goldwater referred to "our wives" feeling unsafe on the street. Such references are similar to those of Whites from the not-so-distant past who overtly decried the black rapist and declared the duty of all White men to protect the White woman. As subsequent conservative policies mushroomed, a harsher justice system was viewed as the solution to the crime problem. Miller contends that "the centerpiece of law enforcement was its preoccupation with highly visible groups who could be relatively easily and publicly arrested. The crown jewel was the handcuffed black youth or young man paraded before TV cameras so all might behold this symbol of lawlessness and disorder" (Miller, 1996, pp. 174–175).

In the 1980s and 1990s, American society, influenced by conservative scholars funded by conservative think tanks, initiated a crusade against crime and drugs. To galvanize the nation's will to combat these evils, a sufficient number of demons, savages, and psychopaths had to be created or uncovered (Miller, 1996). One scholar began to discuss the "super predator" (Marx, 1998), implying that African American juveniles constituted a new breed of criminals. The increased handling of juveniles has had a pejorative effect on African American juveniles sanctioned by the juvenile justice system (Feld, 1995). For example, a recent study showed that African American juveniles are six times more likely to be locked up than White juveniles, although the juveniles commit similar crimes and have similar records (McQueen, 2000).

Despite the specious belief that juveniles are treated leniently by the juvenile justice system, African American juveniles have always been sanctioned severely by the juvenile justice system (Alexander & Gyamerah, 1997). The increased number of African American juveniles in the justice system has led to charges of racial discrimination—a charge strongly denied by many professionals, politicians, and juvenile justice officials (Larson, 1988; Meyer, 1989). Persons who disagree that African American juveniles are handled discriminatorily point to the high number of African Americans participating in serious crimes, such as drug selling and gang activities (Jones, 1996; Wilbanks, 1985). But these charges are a cover for discriminatory policies. The aim of this chapter is to discuss how African American juveniles are treated discriminatorily by the justice system.

The Fallacy of Leniency toward Juveniles and Particularly African American Juveniles

In 1899, the first juvenile court was created in Chicago, Illinois, and a number of other states followed and created their own juvenile courts. Prior to the creation of the juvenile courts, juveniles were treated as adults and tried in adult courts. When the juvenile courts were created, *some* juveniles were tried in juvenile courts. Theoretically, it was possible for juveniles to be tried in juvenile courts for serious offenses, such as murder, rape, robbery, and aggravated assault. However, the early historical records reveal that a significant number of juveniles, even after the creation of the juvenile courts, were treated as adults when accused of serious crimes (Alexander, 1997).

The available records that illustrate the above thesis are execution records in the twentieth century. While social class undoubtedly was a factor in the handling of juveniles, race also played a prominent role in how some juveniles were handled (Streib, 1987). The United States has always looked askance at

African Americans and controlling and oppressing them were paramount. Thus, an African American who offended Whites was targeted for significant and extreme sanctions, regardless of the age and gender of the African American juvenile. The record is replete with instances of young African Americans being executed in what were suspicious and questionable cases.

Accused African American juveniles could have been tried in juvenile court, but a juvenile court judge or prosecutor regularly decided to try them as adults—a process often called waiver or concurrent jurisdiction. Concurrent jurisdiction refers to the discretion given to prosecutors whether to prosecute a young individual in juvenile or adult court. For instance, Virginia in the early 1900s defined a juvenile as a child who was under eighteen years of age (*Brown v. Commonwealth*, 1926; *Cunningham v. Town of Narrows*, 1928; *Ex parte Mallory*, 1918). However, juveniles were frequently tried as adults in Virginia (*Durrette v. Commonwealth of Virginia*, 1960; *Thompson v. Commonwealth*, 1921; *Wansley v. Commonwealth of Virginia*, 1964).

The foremost authority on juvenile executions in the United States, Victor Strieb (1987), presented the ages and races of juveniles who had been executed since slavery until the 1980s. Focusing just on the twentieth century since the creation of the first juvenile court, Alabama, which did not execute any White teenagers, executed five African American juveniles; Arkansas executed five teenagers, of which four were African Americans, and one juvenile's race was undetermined; Florida executed twelve juveniles and eleven of them were African Americans; Georgia executed thirty-four juveniles and thirty-two were African Americans; Kentucky executed seven juveniles and six were African Americans; Louisiana executed six and all were African Americans; Maryland executed three and all were African Americans; Mississippi executed six, and five were African Americans and one juvenile's race was undetermined; North Carolina executed sixteen juveniles and fifteen were African Americans; South Carolina executed eight juveniles and seven were African Americans; Tennessee executed seven and six were African Americans; and Virginia executed fifteen juveniles and all were African Americans (Strieb, 1987).

Some of these cases are striking. For instance, in 1927 Florida executed Fortune Ferguson, who was about thirteen at the time of the alleged crime (Strieb, 1987). No appeal was filed in the Ferguson case except for a legal effort to determine where Ferguson was to be kept prior to the execution and how he was to be executed (*Ferguson v. The State of Florida*, 1925). In 1912, Virginia executed a sixteen-year-old African American female, and in 1943, Georgia executed a seventeen-year-old African American female. In 1944, South Carolina executed a fourteen-year-old African American male, whose story was later depicted in a television movie. Noticeably, many of these

African American juveniles were charged with crimes at one age and executed at the same age. This reveals that these death sentences were not appealed. Further, a search of the legal databases for these states confirms that no appeals existed for them.

A review of existing death penalty cases involving African American juveniles reveals extreme injustices in how these cases may have been handled. As a way of illustration, Preston Cobb, then fifteen years old, was accused of killing a White farmer who employed him in a small rural county. Both Cobb and his mother worked for the farmer, and there were reports that the farmer had repeatedly threatened him. Cobb was convicted and sentenced to die in Georgia's electric chair. After the verdict, Cobb's court-appointed attorney quit the case. Cobb's new attorneys challenged the court-appointed attorney's lack of objection to the composition of the grand jury and trial jury.

The trial occurred in Jasper County, which was 53 percent African American, with 46 percent of them over the age of twenty-one. According to one official's account, no African American had served on a grand jury or trial jury in his thirty years in public office. Further, no one could say that any African American had served on a jury in that county. Yet no White lawyer had ever raised this issue prior to trial. Cobb's original court-appointed attorney stated that he had represented between 200 and 350 African Americans charged with felonies. Furthermore, this attorney charged that he had never felt that any of his African American clients had not received a fair trial because only Whites were permitted to serve on juries. Moreover, he felt it was useless to raise the issue, and even if two or three African Americans served on Cobb's jury, the outcome would have been much worse (*Cobb v. The State*, 1962). At the federal level, the issue of the racial composition was argued again by Cobb's new attorney, and Cobb received a new trial. Subsequent trials resulted in a life sentence, and Cobb served his sentence at the maximum security prison in Reidsville, Georgia (Alexander, 2001).

These cases involve African American juveniles under a significant threat of execution, but a number of cases resulted in life imprisonment. As an illustration, in 1945, three African American males, aged fifteen, sixteen, and seventeen, were accused of robbing and killing a store owner in Ohio. The fifteen-year-old was interrogated from midnight until 5:00 a.m. by several officers. There was evidence that he was beaten by the officers, and, at the end of the interrogation, he signed a confession. Neither his mother nor his attorney was permitted to see him for five days after his arrest. Although the Ohio Supreme Court found this process lawful, the U.S. Supreme Court reversed the fifteen-year-old's conviction and life sentence (*Haley v. Ohio*, 1948).

The picture presented above reflects that African American juveniles were not "slapped on the wrist" when accused of major crimes. While some of the juveniles may have been guilty, many of them likely were not guilty. All these juveniles were accused of killing, raping, or attempting to rape White persons. Often, these juveniles were beaten and intimidated into signing confessions. Even if some punishment was deserved in some cases, often it was extreme. For example, in Botetourt County, Virginia, a group of White and African American boys were involved in a dispute. According to the African American defendant, the White boys had threatened to run him out of town. Shortly thereafter, one of the White boys threw a firecracker that exploded over the head of the African American boy, who then fired a weapon at them. He shot four White boys, one of whom died. A White mob was threatening to lynch the African American boy, and he ran. When apprehended, the African American was shot. When he went to trial, the jury convicted him and sentenced him to die in the electric chair (*Thompson v. Commonwealth*, 1921). While there was some provocation, this case did not warrant the death penalty. This case was more manslaughter than it was murder. Undoubtedly, if it were reversed and an African American boy threatened and threw an exploding firecracker at a White boy, a subsequent homicide would not lead to the death penalty for a White boy.

A somewhat forgotten symbol of how African American juveniles were handled by the justice system is reflected by the case of the "Scottsboro Boys." This was a case from the 1930s in Alabama that involved a racial conflict. Nine African American youths, the oldest being nineteen, were riding a gondola car to look for work during the Great Depression. A group of Whites, including two females, got on the gondola and ordered the African Americans off, adhering to the principle of separation of the races and white supremacy. The African Americans refused and a fight ensued in which all the Whites were thrown off the gondola. Upon leaving the train, the Whites went to the sheriff, claiming that a gang of African Americans had attacked them. Law enforcement was telegraphed ahead, told to stop the train, and arrest all the African Americans. All were subsequently charged with rape. Although the prosecutor never called the White males to support the allegation of rape and one White female recanted the rape allegation, the African Americans were all convicted and some were given death sentences or lengthy prison sentences. One defendant went on trial three times, receiving two death sentences and finally a sentence of about eighty years (*Patterson v. Alabama*, 1935).

The historical record is full of cases involving racial conflict in which African Americans received unjust treatment, either as defendants or victims. Yet, opponents of the view that racial injustices exist in the legal system do not acknowledge any past problems with race and justice. If one or two opponents acknowledge past racial injustices, they are very quick to state that the past is gone and no racial injustices exist today. They charge that African American youth are more involved in gang violence, drugs, and violent crimes, accounting for their high involvement in the legal system. However, research does not support these officials' accounts.

A More Contemporary Analysis of African American Juveniles in the Justice System

As the populations of correctional institutions increased in the 1970s, one of the salient features that emerged was that African Americans' involvement in the justice system rose dramatically and was quite disconcerting given the percentage of African Americans in the total U.S. population. This "disproportionate" chasm prompted debate about the reason for this racial disparity (Dunn, Cernkovich, Perry, & Wicks, 1993; Feld, 1995). On one hand, some professionals charge racism within the justice system. On the other hand, some professionals explain African Americans' involvement in the justice system by African Americans' high participation in crimes of violence that are targeted by the justice system and public involvement in crack cocaine. Other persons split the argument down the middle and say the truth is a little of both (Chambers, 1995; Walker, Spohn, & Delone, 1996; Wolfgang, 1970).

The author of this chapter argues that the charge of racism is more correct. Juveniles who are involved in highly sensational crimes are going to be handled toughly regardless of the race of the juvenile. Shooting up a school classroom and killing fellow students or mutilating one's parents and siblings is going to be met with tough sanctions. These types of crimes generally involve White juveniles, especially the recent school shootings since 1998 (Wise, 2001; Zuckerman, 1999). The FBI has created a profile of school shooters and has cautioned teachers to be observant of some "geeks" ("FBI Lists Caution Signs," 2000). Deniers of racism in the justice system likely will point to these cases and the lengthy sentences given as evidence that White youths are not given special considerations by the justice system.

The problem with this type of argument is that extreme violence by juveniles is a rare phenomenon given the juvenile delinquency problem. The question is what happens to juveniles who are charged with lesser offenses, such as possessing drugs, stealing, shoplifting, disorderly conduct, and assaults. In these areas, and especially in the area of drug offenses, racism is quite apparent.

A number of researchers have examined the issue of the overrepresentation of African Americans in the juvenile justice system and have concluded that this issue can no longer be denied (Feyerherm, 1995; Pope, 1995). Originally, conservatives contended that African Americans were more likely to commit serious offenses, and this fact explained why they were more likely to be incarcerated and sanctioned. However, this contention was questioned and rejected. For instance, the most serious crimes are index crimes, also called Part 1 offenses. These consist of homicide, aggravated assault, rape, burglary, auto theft, arson, and larceny-theft. In that these are the most serious offenses, juveniles who commit these offenses, in theory, are more likely to be committed. However, this theoretical framework is not supported. White adolescents are more likely to be arrested for rape, burglary, auto theft, and larceny, but the institutionalized juvenile population does not reflect this pattern. More simply, if African Americans constitute 53 percent of all juveniles arrested for homicides, they should constitute roughly that percentage of juveniles incarcerated. If White juveniles constitute more than 40 percent of the juveniles arrested for homicide, something is wrong if they constitute less than 20 percent of those incarcerated for homicides.

In 2002, 8,176,791 arrests were made involving juveniles less than eighteen years of age (Federal Bureau of Investigation, 2004). Of this total, 5,764,614 (71 percent) arrests involved White juveniles and 2,217,778 (27 percent) involved African American juveniles (Federal Bureau of Investigation, 2004). In terms of violent crimes, 61 percent of these arrests were of White juveniles, compared to 37 percent of African American juveniles (Federal Bureau of Investigation, 2004). For property offenses, 67 percent of these arrests involved White juveniles and 31 percent involved African American juveniles (Federal Bureau of Investigation, 2004). White juveniles constituted 61 percent of the arrests for carrying or possessing weapons, compared to 38 percent being African American juveniles (Federal Bureau of Investigation, 2004). White juveniles made up 65 percent of the arrests for drug abuse violations, compared to 34 percent for African American juveniles (Federal Bureau of Investigation, 2004). Hence, the raw data do not support the high concentration of African American juveniles.

Buttressing the raw data, a number of multivariate studies have been conducted that soundly conclude that racial discrimination exists in the justice system involving African American juveniles. In California, James Austin (1995) studied the overrepresentation of minorities in state juvenile facilities. Utilizing the Office of Juvenile Justice and Delinquency Prevention's recommendation, Austin used the Minority Proportion Index and Minority Incarceration Rate. The Minority Proportion Index was calculated by dividing the percentage of youth in a minority group incarcerated by the California Youth Authority by the percentage of youth in that group in the state of California. Obviously, anything greater than 1 represents overrepresentation. The Minority Incarceration Rate is the number of minorities incarcerated per 100,000 group members in that state. As reported by Austin, for males, African

Americans had an index of 4.25 and a rate of 1,950 per 100,000; Latinos had an index of .94 and a rate of 430 per 100,000; Asians had an index of .65 and a rate of 295 per 100,000; and Whites had an index of .99 and a rate of 449 per 100,000. For females, African Americans had an index of .58 and rate of 272 per 100,000; Whites had an index of .15 and a rate of 69 per 100,000; Latinos had an index of .12 and a rate of 53 per 100,000; Asians had an index of .08 and a rate of 32 per 100,000. Austin concluded that African American juveniles receive more severe dispositions throughout the process, "even when this and other relevant factors are controlled for" (Austin, 1995, p. 177). Implied in this conclusion is that the severity of offense and the previous record cannot explain these racial differences, and race, thus, is the primary factor involved.

In the state of Washington, a group of researchers studied racial disparities in several counties, examining crime and social structure variables. They depicted and tested a comprehensive model of racial incarceration rates. In addition, they buttressed their quantitative analyses with qualitative analyses. The researchers analyzed White and minority juveniles separately, focusing upon referral rates, violent crime, minority concentration, economic inequality, urban concentration, and court workload. Rate of referral to court was significant for White youth, but not for minorities. The researchers stated that "it would be erroneous to conclude that racial disparities in confinement are primarily or solely the result of differential rates of arrest and referral of minority youth. Clearly, rates of referral for minorities are poor predictors of minorities in confinement across Washington counties" (Bridges, Conley, Engen, & Price-Spratlen, 1995, p. 144). In addition, minority juveniles' involvement in violent crime was strongly associated with the rate of juvenile confinement, but not for White juveniles. The researchers suggested that whether a county had a high rate of violence was a stronger predictor of confinement (Bridges et al., 1995).

However, another interpretation of this finding is that violent crime participation is not significant in predicting White youth incarceration because White youth are more likely to receive alternative dispositions when they have committed violent crimes. Because the data were analyzed separately and because violent crime is a matter of societal concern, violent crimes should be a predictor for both White and minority youth's incarceration. Because it was not a significant predictor for White youth, a fair interpretation is that a significant number of White youth that have been adjudicated delinquent for violent crime receive dispositions other than incarceration.

A recent study in Washington seems to support the above interpretation. In this study, two researchers studied probation officers' written records and reports to juvenile court judges to assess the impact of race and probation officers' assessment. Coding various information in these written documents, the researchers were able to glean the extent of environmental influences, the extent of a delinquent personality, the level of negative external attributions, and the degree of negative internal attributions. They found that probation officers consistently attributed African American and White juveniles' delinquency to different factors. African American juveniles were more likely to have their delinquency attributed to negative attitudinal and personality traits, whereas White juveniles' delinquency was attributed to the social environment. How juveniles were assessed was important in determining the degree of threat to a community and the type of recommended sentence. Simply, juveniles who were deemed threats to the community were more likely to have a negative probation report prepared. Upon seeing "red flags," judges were more likely to treat African American juveniles harshly than White juveniles. More importantly, the courts gave more weight to those cases with "red flags" than the severity of the offense or prior criminal record (Bridges & Steen, 1998).

Bridges et al. (1995), upon interviewing juvenile justice officials, uncovered the standard explanations for minority overrepresentation, which the data refuted. The researchers reported that "many officials viewed disparities in confinement as an unfortunate consequence of disproportionate minority involvement in serious and violent crimes. Although empirical evidence presented in this chapter does not support the view that disparities in confinement are caused by differential minority involvement in crime, many officials felt that their communities had experienced a recent increase in crime rates among youth and that much of the increase in violent crimes had occurred among youths and that much of the increase in violent crimes had occurred among youths of color. Many felt that this escalated level of violence contributed to increased likelihood of racial differences in arrest, adjudication, and confinement to correctional facilities" (p. 149).

In Florida, Charles Frazier and Donna Bishop (1995) carried out a study authorized by the Florida Supreme Commission on race and ethnic bias. They were interested in four dependent variables—intake screening, detention status, court referral, and judicial disposition. They utilized a number of predictor or independent variables, including race, gender, age, prior record, offense severity, and detention status. Following their analyses, they concluded that "our quantitative analyses indicate that non-White juveniles referred for delinquency offenses in Florida receive more severe (i.e., more formal and/or more restrictive) dispositions than their White counterparts at each of the four stages in processing. Specifically, after controls are introduced for age, gender, seriousness of the referral offense, and seriousness of their prior records, we find significant race effects. The magnitude of the race effect ranges between 4 and 7 percentages points at four decision points, with some indirect effects working through detention decisions" (p. 27).

In Pennsylvania, Leonard and Sontheimer (1995) studied the influence of race in juvenile decision making. They acknowledged that their results were complicated and not easily interpretable. Nonetheless, they concluded African American and Latino juveniles were more likely to receive formal processing than White juveniles, controlling for offense, prior record, and school problems. In addition, African American and Latino juveniles were more likely to be detained than similarly situated White juveniles. The data showed that "minority status seemed to be accorded more importance at detention than even person-related offenses; any personal, family, or school problem; location; referral source; or court caseload. The race effect with detention and the subsequent importance of detention suggest that an indirect race effect also may result in adjudication and placement more often for minorities, and especially for blacks" (p. 120).

In Michigan, some researchers studied factors affecting police decision making, i.e., whether to divert or arrest (Wordes & Bynum, 1995). As in many of the other studies described above, these researchers used logistic regression to analyze their data. According to them, race and ethnicity "played a significant and independent role in the referral and custody decisions made by police officers. White youths were more likely than black youths to be dropped, diverted, or released at the scene, controlling for offense seriousness and prior offenses. Similarly, black youths were more likely to be referred to court, and to be detained" (p. 62).

Looking at some of these statistics on the overrepresentation of African American juveniles in the justice system, I (Alexander, 1996) speculated that the country's drug policy was partly responsible. Compounding this problem was that African American juveniles were targeted by the justice system, whereas White juveniles were not, despite a plethora of studies that showed that White adolescents used more drugs than African Americans. In one study I reviewed, Georgia had one hundred youths in confinement for drug offenses, and all were African Americans. In the suburbs around Cleveland, Ohio, White juveniles were arrested for drugs, but their offenses were handled informally instead of being taken to juvenile detention. A suburban committee existed in these communities and these communities would decide what to do with the White juveniles. Based on the injustice to African American juveniles, I advocated that African American juveniles who have only drug offenses be treated by their communities from a mental health perspective with no legal involvement (Alexander, 1996).

Conclusion

The influence of race can be seen in a debate regarding Michigan's juvenile justice law. Michigan has one of the most punitive laws in the country regarding the treatment of adolescents and children who commit crimes. It has among its provisions that a child regardless of his or her age can be charged as an adult. One state legislator contended that the law is aimed at juveniles who commit serious crimes, such as murder and rape. If the child is convicted, the judge may impose a juvenile sentence, or a blended sentence consisting of some confinement in a juvenile facility and some time in an adult facility once the juvenile has turned twenty-one. Another sentencing option is that the juvenile could be sentenced to life imprisonment without parole with part of the sentence served in the juvenile system and the remaining time in the adult prison system. In 1999, this law was used to try and convict a thirteen-year-old African American boy who was accused of a murder that he was alleged to have committed when he was eleven years old.

While this actual Michigan trial involving this thirteen-year-old does not have racial overtones, the system reflects racism. By way of illustration, about six or seven months before this trial, a debate had ensued in Michigan regarding whether the juvenile law was too harsh. Moreover, some judges were commenting that this law was too harsh, prompting one judge to rule Michigan's juvenile law unconstitutional, setting up an appeal to the Michigan Court of Appeals (Truby, 1999a; Truby, 1999b). What prompted these discussions were three juvenile cases involving White juveniles (Truby, 1999c).

When this law was passed, the legislature sought to permit juveniles who committed serious crimes, such as murder and armed robbery, to be tried as adults and not as juveniles. Undoubtedly, when the state legislators had in mind the prevention of juveniles who committed murder or armed robbery being slapped on the wrist in the juvenile justice system, they saw black adolescents. But when the law threatened White middle-class adolescents with life imprisonment without parole for the same crimes, Michigan juvenile justice law became too harsh and legally suspect in some people's views. The Michigan Court of Appeals did not rule that life without parole for a juvenile was unconstitutional, but the current debate smacks of racism. None of these individuals who now believe the law is too harsh said so when African American juveniles were being tried as adults and sentenced to adult prisons. A middle-class African American juvenile would not receive the same concern or compassion that was being shown for three White middle-class adolescents. This practice shows again that if the legal system is giving out breaks, these breaks will not be distributed fairly. In the juvenile justice system, White adolescents are going to receive the greatest proportion of the breaks, and African Americans are going to receive less.

4

African Americans, Maltreatment, and Law Enforcement

CIVIL DISOBEDIENCE HAS LONG occurred in American society, resulting some-times in riots. Large gatherings of Whites have stormed jails and lynched African Americans. These behaviors were unnecessary because juries really never acquitted African Americans who were accused of serious offenses against Whites, and the typical outcome was the death penalty in a very short time span. During the birth of the labor movement, aspiring union members fought law enforcement officers, who often were controlled by major indus-tries and ordered to put down disobedient workers. Similarly, miners have re-volted against mineowners over working conditions and low pay. Likewise, African Americans have shown their displeasure with their treatment and have engaged in civil disobedience and rioting.

Contrary to other groups, whenever African Americans rioted in this coun-try, the primary causal factor was the maltreatment of them by law enforce-ment officials. The infamous Watts riots in 1966 occurred after African Amer-icans became enraged over the rough treatment of an African American woman by police officers of the Los Angeles Police Department (Raine, 1967). Later, the beating of Rodney King, an African American, and the acquittal of the White officers involved sparked a deadly riot. From coast to coast, civil dis-obedience and riots have occurred when police officers have killed African Americans, used brutality in making arrests, or caused the deaths mysteri-ously of African Americans in jails (Chaney & Carrillo, 1999).

Human Rights Watch, an international investigating body that monitors and condemns human rights violations, recognizes police brutality as a viola-tion of U.S. citizens' rights. According to Human Rights Watch, "police officers engage in unjustified shootings, severe beatings, fatal choking, and unnecessary rough physical treatment in cities throughout the United States, while their police superiors, city officials, and the Justice Department fail to act decisively to restrain or penalize such acts or even to record the full magnitude of the problem" (Collins, 1998, p. 1).

The aim of this chapter is to discuss incidents of maltreatment by law enforcement against African Americans. The current maltreatment of African Americans by law enforcement officers consists of two forms of ill treatment —excessive force and unjustified stops. Both excessive force and unjustified stops may take several forms. Excessive force involves death, shootings, and beatings, whereas unjustified stops may be what African Americans call DWB or Driving While Black, or simply being stopped on the streets. The focus here is on excessive force and unnecessary car stops because these constitute the law enforcement activities that generate the most consternation by African Americans.

Background of the Problem

As with other areas, the maltreatment of African Americans by law enforcement officers has a long history. After slavery, the Black Codes were established and law enforcement officers carried out their enforcement. At about the same time, the Ku Klux Klan emerged and often law enforcement officers were members of the Klan. Because law enforcement officers failed to do their jobs and often were instrumental in helping to prevent African Americans from exercising basic civil rights, Congress passed the Civil Rights Act of 1871. This law, which is still on the books, speaks in part about officials acting "under the color of law," holding them civilly liable for civil rights violations. Essentially, a law enforcement officer, acting under a racist law, could still be liable to African Americans for depriving them of basic rights. This 1871 act was revised to include criminal penalties for the violation of citizens' rights. Because the states would not protect African Americans, this was the principal tool used against the Ku Klux Klan and White officials for about 100 years. However, it was seldom used for a number of years. Sporadically, it was used to try and convict several members of the Ku Klux Klan, including the sheriff and his deputies, for the killing of the three civil rights workers in Mississippi in the 1960s (*United States v. Price et al.*, 1966). Later, it was used to convict members of the Los Angeles Police Department who beat Rodney King.

Besides controlling and preventing African Americans from exercising basic rights, law enforcement was brutal in its treatment of African American citizens. In an extraordinary exercise, in 1964 a lawsuit was filed in Mississippi charging law enforcement officers in every county of violating the civil rights of African Americans. The plaintiffs requested a federal officer in every sheriff's office in every county. In support of this lawsuit, a number of notarized affidavits were filed detailing African Americans' maltreatment. Most of the affidavits involved individuals who were involved in some capacity with civil rights and voter registration. Thus, to Mississippi lawmen, these were rebellious behaviors that needed to be eradicated.

However, routine brutality occurred against African Americans who were not involved in civil rights behaviors that incited White Mississippians. For instance, a twenty-one-year-old African American female stated that she was walking down a street in Clarksdale, Mississippi, when two officers stopped her and accused her of being involved in a theft. According to the woman, "I was taken to jail by the officers and they forced me to unclothe and lie on my back. One of the officers beat me between my legs with a belt. A few minutes later, the other officer began to beat me across my naked breasts" (Niebuhr, 1965, p. 6). This incident occurred on February 6, 1962, a period before civil rights demonstrations occurred in Mississippi, and suggested that brutality against African Americans was a common occurrence among law enforcement officers. Many lawmen saw nothing wrong with beating confessions from African Americans accused of crimes. As one Mississippi sheriff reported, beatings were customary in the county jail to initiate new prisoners, and the sheriff did not see anything wrong with the beating of a Black man who confessed to murder after repeated beatings while unclothed and was subsequently sentenced to die (*Whip v. State,* 1926).

However not all maltreatment occurred in Mississippi or the South. In fact, maltreatment by law enforcement officials of African Americans occurred nationwide and within the context of maltreatment of accused offenders in general. Called "the third degree," a number of law enforcement practices were designed to coerce confessions and punish offenders extralegally. As an illustration, Emanuel Lavine (1930), a crime reporter, disclosed the brutal tactics used by law enforcement officers in New York City to get people to confess to crimes. Torture and beatings were routinely administered to suspects. One African American, who had been accused of killing a police officer, was thrown headfirst down some stone stairs and sustained massive head injuries. Because the injuries were so severe, he could not be tried and was committed to an institution for the criminally insane (Lavine, 1930).

In 1999, a New Jersey state trooper was killed. Several African American suspects were arrested. One African American contended that he was kept in jail for six days before he was cleared. During this six-day period, he contended that several masked officers beat him. Another African American man, who was arrested as a suspect in the trooper's killing, died in police custody

(Fallon, 1999). Although officers were known to use more brutality when an officer was killed or assaulted, extreme brutality was used in other cases to secure confessions in weak or nonexistent cases.

Thus, law enforcement officers have been instrumental in controlling African Americans in this country. Often, they were given support in using heavy-handed tactics in the ghettos. All African Americans were viewed as criminals. They could be stopped and questioned without suspicion of a crime being committed, arrested en masse and held on open charges, beaten and tortured in the jails, and killed under suspicious circumstances. Often, there was no punishment for the officers. As a result, civil disturbances have occurred by African Americans. Although violence by law enforcement has abated, maltreatment has not ceased. African Americans are still more likely to be beaten, killed, and stopped without good cause (Suro, 1999).

Tom Owens, a former officer for the Los Angles Police Department for twelve years, created a private investigation business and worked for the attorney who initially represented Rodney King following King's beating by members of the Los Angeles Police Department. Owens, who is White, wrote a book in which he described the racism in the Los Angeles Police Department that would permit an atmosphere in which officers felt comfortable in mistreating African Americans. Owens wrote, "an officer assigned to a minority area too often undergoes a transformation in attitude. More often than not, the officer will choose a stricter interpretation and a tougher course of action than he would in a 'better' neighborhood. Most African Americans have known this for years. Everyone else saw it—perhaps for the first time—in the Holliday video" [i.e., the infamous beating of Rodney King] (Owens, 1994, p. 10). Furthermore, Owens, showing the racism in the department, stated that sometimes the acronym NVNNHI appeared in police records. This means "Nigger versus Nigger—No Human Involved." As a result, there is no crime and no need to take it seriously.

Excessive Force

Few African Americans would deny that law enforcement officers have the right and duty to shoot some individuals. An armed African American who is holding hostages may have to be killed. Also, an African American who has just robbed a store and is shooting at officers may have to be killed too. However, other types of shooting are not justified. These would be shooting an unarmed and fleeing African American in the back; shooting someone who is unarmed and lying on the ground; or shooting an individual, although armed with an object, when the officers are some distance away and not imminently threatened.

Also, an unjustified use of force is beating a suspect when it is unnecessary to effect an arrest and is only done for punishment. For instance, part of the reason for members of the Los Angeles Police Department beating Rodney King was that he would not initially stop his car and later taunted the officers. If true, these behaviors still do not justify the beating that Rodney King received.

A police officer has no authority to administer punishment in this society. The officers had more than enough support to effect an arrest of King, but they wanted to punish him for running from them and taunting them. Young White adolescents steal cars and sometimes engage law enforcement officers in high-speed chases. When caught, they sometimes express disdain for law enforcement. However, law enforcement takes a different approach with these types of offenders. In a similar fashion, a mentally disturbed White female who is armed with a knife and a mentally disturbed African American female armed with a knife are treated differently by law enforcement officers. The officers may be more patient with the White female and are not likely to shoot her. However, the African American female may be shot and killed. These differences in treatment constitute racism.

For instance, in 1979, Ms. Eulia May Love, an African American, had a dispute with the gas company over a gas bill for $22.09. Two members of the Los Angeles Police Department went to her house. Upon the officers' arrival, Ms. Love was trying to cut two small trees in her front yard with a knife. Ms. Love was ordered to put the knife down, but she was agitated and did not immediately comply. Two minutes and twenty-seven seconds after arriving at Ms. Love's home, Ms. Love was dead from eight gunshots (Domanick, 1999). The officers claimed that they felt threatened by her, but both the Assistant Chief and a Police Commission investigating the death concluded that the officers were not reasonable and the situation was handled poorly (Domanick, 1999). Investigating officials concluded that what likely happened was that the officers became quickly annoyed at Ms. Love screaming at them and shot her for challenging them (Domanick, 1999).

The Love case was retrieved from Los Angelenos' memories because a similar killing of an African American woman occurred in Los Angeles in 1999. Ms. Margaret Mitchell, a college-educated, mentally disturbed woman who became mentally ill and homeless, was stopped on the streets to be questioned about a stolen shopping cart. The officers shot and killed Ms. Mitchell when they claimed she had threatened them with a screwdriver (Domanick, 1999). Within a three-year period in Southern California, five African American females were killed by law enforcement officers (Hutchinson, 1999). Utilizing a takeoff of the "force" in the latest "Star Wars" movie, Derrick (1999) advises that African Americans experience a different "force" than Whites and all African Americans, including women, fear when the "force" is in their neighborhood.

One of the more highly publicized recent incidents of excessive force occurred in New York. A West African resident was shot at forty-one times by four White officers with nineteen bullets striking and killing the man, Amadou Diallo (Jacoby, 1999). In another recent case, an African American computer salesman in New Jersey who allegedly rocked his car forward and backward on a New Jersey Turnpike after he was stopped was shot at twenty-seven times by four officers and killed by numerous shots (Fallon, 1999). In 1998, several officers, seeking to punish a man named Abner Louima—who incidentally was the wrong man—for striking them during an arrest at a nightclub, beat the man in a precinct restroom and forced a stick into the victim's rectum. Taking the stick out of the victim's rectum, one officer jammed the stick into the victim's mouth. The victim suffered severe internal injuries as the result of the assault (Fried, 1998).

Prompted by a White man murdering his pregnant wife and his falsely accusing an African American, the St. Clair Commission in Boston found most complaints regarding police brutality in the city were made by African Americans although African Americans constituted 25 percent of the population (Collins, 1998). This murder case in Boston illustrates why African Americans make a high proportion of complaints of police brutality. Although the case was horrendous, it was made more sensitive because an African American male was alleged to have killed a pregnant White woman. The White and law enforcement community in Boston was highly incensed and developed a lynch-mob-type attitude. Numerous African Americans were arrested and the police moved into the African American community without regard to the rights of residents. Police officers made door-to-door searches of African Americans' houses and roughed up people who protested. In addition, almost every African American male was stopped on the street on the chance that he might be the offender or know something about the crime (Collins, 1998).

If a White perpetrator of this crime had been alleged, the White community and law enforcement community still would have been upset. However, the difference is that the police would not have moved into a predominately White neighborhood, treating everyone as if he or she were a suspect or collaborator and roughing up people who protested. Essentially, the U.S. Constitution was deemed not to apply to African Americans' homes. The police officers needed not to get search warrants or have probable cause to go into an African American's house. This would not be done in a White neighborhood.

Racial Profiling, Stops, and Their Effects

The practice of racial profiling has come under attack by African Americans and others (Browne, 1998; Deutsch, 1999; Hudson, 2000; Meredith, 2000).

Racial profiling is the practice of establishing characteristics of offenders, with race as a primary factor. Such profiling may be established by sophisticated statistical modeling, such as predicting what type of parolees are more likely to offend. Age might be one variable, along with the type of crime, social class, gender, and race. Profiling can be more simple, which is what is generally done, and involves stopping all African Americans who are driving late model cars. Law enforcement officers accused of racial profiling have created a system for stopping cars that may be suspected of carrying drugs or contraband, and many of these officers making the stops are White males (Woodards & Brand-Williams, 2000). A stop is made and then evidence is looked for in plain view. Also, the demeanor of the driver or passenger may come under suspicion. Once suspicion is aroused, a drug dog may be summoned to the scene, providing the probable cause to make a full search. The problem with such practices is that if the profile is limited to just African American or Latino drivers, then, of course, most arrests are going to occur with African Americans or Latinos. Whites carrying drugs are not stopped according to the profile.

Supporters of law enforcement's aggressive practices with African Americans point to the high rate of African Americans involved in violent crimes and drug activities (McCarthy, 1999). To these supporters, stopping, frisking, and profiling African Americans make sound law enforcement practices. However, these arguments are quite weak and unsupported. Without a doubt, African Americans are involved in crimes at a rate higher than their percentage in the population. But this does not mean that African Americans commit all the crimes, as supporters of law enforcement insinuate.

For instance, crimes are ranked according to seriousness, and the most serious crimes are called index crimes. These are murder, forcible rape, robbery, aggravated assault, burglary, larceny-theft, motor vehicle theft, and arson. For 2002, 1,620,594 arrests were made, according to the Federal Bureau of Investigation (2004). Of this total, 1,158,776 were White and 415,854 were African American (Federal Bureau of Investigation, 2004). Whites were arrested for 55 percent of the violent crimes and African Americans were arrested for 43 percent of them (Federal Bureau of Investigation, 2004). In addition, Whites were arrested for 70 percent of property crimes, whereas African Americans were arrested for 27 percent of them (Federal Bureau of Investigation, 2004). For the most serious crimes, about 46 percent of those arrested for murder and nonnegligent manslaughter were White and 50 percent of those arrested were African American; for forcible rape 62 percent were White and 36 percent were African American; for robbery 39 percent were White and 59 percent were African American; for aggravated assault 61 percent were White and 37 percent were African American; for burglary 72 percent were White and 25 percent were African American; for larceny-theft 70 percent were White and 27 percent were African Americans; for motor vehicle theft 58 percent were White and 38 percent were African American; for Arson 81 percent were White and 18 percent were African American (Federal Bureau of Investigation, 2004).

The news media often highlight African Americans' involvement in carrying weapons and involvement with drugs. For carrying or possessing weapons, 25,239 persons were arrested in 2002 (Federal Bureau of Investigation, 2004). Of this total, 67 percent were White and 31 percent were African Americans (Federal Bureau of Investigation, 2004). Also, in 2002, 133,494 persons were arrested for drug abuse violations (Federal Bureau of Investigation, 2004). Whites made up 73 percent of those arrested for drug abuse, compared to 25 percent for African Americans (Federal Bureau of Investigation, 2004).

From these statistics, one can conclude that racial profiling is more practical for Whites. Maybe, if a storeowner was found murdered and a robbery occurred, law enforcement might look at African American suspects first. But for other crimes, Whites should be looked at first. Thus, if a police department wanted to catch motor vehicle thieves, they should profile Whites and stop them at random for proof of title. In addition, if they were looking for weapon violations, more Whites should be stopped and frisked. But this is not what is done.

Instead, African Americans are targeted as criminogenic. This means that innocent African Americans are more likely to be stopped than innocent Whites. It also means that a higher percentage of guilty Whites is permitted to escape detection because they are not profiled. Consider this illustration: several Whites who work on Wall Street are riding in a car with powder cocaine in their possession and an illegal weapon; in another car are several African Americans with crack cocaine and an illegal weapon. An officer sees both cars simultaneously and decides to stop the car with the African Americans because they are known to have drugs and weapons. A pretense stop likely will uncover the drugs and weapons, while the car with the Whites is permitted to go unchecked. Because Whites are arrested for weapons and drugs, their arrests occur for other reasons unrelated to profiling (e.g., there is an accident and the drugs are discovered by chance or there is a planned checkpoint where all cars are stopped or every third car is stopped).

At Ohio State University, an undercover operation learned that one White female student was transporting and bringing heroin to campus. She boasted that she was not afraid to carry drugs because no one would suspect a "White chick." In short, she was saying that she would not be stopped on the interstate or a highway and her car randomly searched for drugs. Her car had an Ohio State parking sticker, identifying her as a student. Thus, she was completely safe from unjustified stops and discovery. She was only stopped when she boasted on campus about her activities and this information reached the undercover officer. In order for her to be caught transporting drugs, she would have to have had an accident and the drugs be found by an officer looking in the car to turn off the ignition switch or trying to get her out. An African American carrying drugs has a higher probability of being stopped.

Stone (1999), presenting a paper to President Clinton's Advisory Board on Race, describes the practices described above and illustrates the negative consequences of racial profiling. A study was conducted of searches made by Maryland state troopers of drivers on Interstate Highway 95. African Americans constituted 17 percent of the drivers on this portion of the interstate and, as expected, 17.5 percent of the speeders cited were African Americans. However, of 533 drivers who were searched, African Americans constituted 409 or 77 percent. Stone poses this question: "Why were black motorists searched so often?" The police might justify such practices on the grounds that blacks are more likely to be carrying contraband. And the statistics show this to be true: the police found contraband in 33 percent of the searches of black motorists and in 22 percent of the searches of White motorists. But the mischief in this practice is quickly exposed. Blacks had a 50 percent higher chance of being found with contraband, but were searched more than 400 percent more often. The result is that 274 innocent black motorists were searched, while only 76 innocent White motorists were searched. The profiles apparently used by the Maryland state troopers make "17 percent of the motorists pay 76 percent of the price of law enforcement strategy, solely because of their race" (p. 28).

In 2004, the state of Massachusetts commenced a probe of racial profiling by ordering the monitoring of all traffic tickets issued in the state by public safety officers. This probe was ordered after a four-year study by professors at Northeastern University that analyzed 1.6 million traffic citations issued in Massachusetts from April 1, 2001, to June 30, 2003. The four evaluative criteria were (1) ticketing resident minorities disproportionately more than Whites; (2) ticketing all minorities disproportionately more than Whites; (3) searching minorities more often than Whites; and (4) giving warnings to Whites more often than minorities. The study involved 366 departments in Massachusetts; 274 departments failed when evaluated regarding the extent to which these departments engaged in racial profiling of minorities ("Massachusetts launches racial profiling probe," 2004).

Despite statistics that show that for crime in general White Americans are more likely to be the perpetrators, many White Americans, including law enforcement, view African Americans as the criminals. A law-abiding African American is very likely to be treated as a criminal. Numerous African American professionals are stopped and treated as if they have just committed a crime. Even African American prosecutors are stopped in some cities without just cause. Chris Darden, one of the prosecutors of O. J. Simpson, stated that he had been stopped without just cause. Dennis Archer, Jr., the son of the mayor of Detroit and a licensed attorney, was stopped, handcuffed, and put in the back of a police cruiser, along with his date, an assistant prosecutor. When he asked why was he stopped and arrested, he was told to shut up. Neither was asked for identification. After learning who Mr. Archer and his date were, the officers told them that they had been looking for a robbery suspect. Upon learning of his son's arrest, the mayor, Dennis Archer, Sr., recalled that in 1985, he was stopped too while driving a Cadillac. Both his car and briefcase were searched. At that time, Mr. Archer, Sr., was president of the State Bar Association. Upon seeing contents in the briefcase that identified Mr. Archer, Sr., as an attorney, the officer apologized and permitted him to leave ("Son of Detroit Mayor Files Complaint," 1999).

An African American police officer in Boston who was on duty and in plainclothes joined a chase of a suspected criminal. Several White officers, believing that the African American police officer was the suspect, stopped this officer and began beating him. The officer sustained a damaged kidney and several cuts about the head and face, requiring transportation to the hospital. The White officers told a number of stories about this incident, saying that the African American officer was not at the scene and was not injured at all. Despite these inconsistencies, the officers were not disciplined or charged for beating their brother officer (Collins, 1998).

Some conservatives have attributed this problem to African Americans who commit crimes and stated that this group should be blamed instead of law enforcement (D'Souza, 1995). This type of explanation is highly racist. Whites commit a number of crimes themselves, and their crimes are not used to justify the ill treatment of middle- and upper-class White Americans. Most mass murderers in this country are White, but law enforcement does not mistreat Whites because of this fact. The crime of Timothy McVeigh, who was convicted of killing over one hundred people, is not used to carry out Gestapo tactics in the White community. Efforts to find the accomplices of McVeigh did not result in widespread illegal searches of Whites.

As stated by Owens, police officers have one mind-set when they go into a middle-class neighborhood and a different mind-set when they go into a minority neighborhood. An officer who goes into a middle- or upper-class White neighborhood because of a loud party is going to act differently than on a similar type of call into a minority neighborhood. In the juvenile justice field, it is alleged that African American youths are more likely to be arrested for trivial charges because these youths are more likely to behave discourteously. They want to stand up to the "man" and show their friends and themselves that they are not afraid of a White police officer. However, there has not been any research to show that White youths are more respectful. In fact, the opposite may be true. White adolescents can be very disrespectful to officers. Further, one theory of deviant behavior indicates that law enforcement is much more likely to act when a minority is behaving deviantly or when challenged by a member of a perceived deviant group. Traditionally, an African American talking back to a White man or looking a White man in the eye was a serious infraction, whereas a White individual who was viewed as a full citizen could express his displeasure toward another White man. A White man has urged another White man to "treat me like a White man," which means do not treat me like a second-class citizen or like a nigger.

Consequences of Excessive Force and Maltreatment

Maltreatment and excessive force have consequences. As Attorney General Janet Reno stated, law enforcement needs the support of the community in fighting crime and excessive force attenuates this needed support (Lichtblau, 1999). Discussing the Abner Louima case, Lawrence Finnegan, a judge for the New York Supreme Court, stated that police brutality cases were not unique or isolated situations. Police brutality, according to Judge Finnegan, has been prevalent in New York for a long time. Although most officers in New York condemned the brutality of the officers in the Louima case, they support a lesser degree of brutality and only feel that the officers went too far with Louima (Finnegan, 1999).

Judge Finnegan cautions that the brutality committed against Louima and others not publicized has very negative consequences for everyone. Quoting Judge Finnegan, "for those who don't see this act of sadism affecting them, just watch as we experience more and more not-guilty verdicts in this city. Cases that seem safe for prosecutors will increasingly result in acquittals as more and more jurors, White as well as others, give the edge to the criminal in those marginal cases turning on police credibility. As a consequence, we all suffer from brutality in a way that affects the very quality of life that the police are supposed to be improving" (Finnegan, 1999, p. 3).

Although Judge Finnegan was clearly referring to a fallout in New York, his comments have nationwide implications. Like New York, Los Angeles has a history of police brutality. Many persons heard first of Johnny Cochran during the O. J. Simpson case, but Johnny Cochran had a long history of fighting police brutality cases in Los Angeles. Nearly twenty years before O. J. Simpson, Johnny Cochran was involved in a case in which reports were that an African American was murdered in jail by law enforcement. African

Americans never forgot this case and others in which police officers had been shown to lie after committing illegal acts. Thus, it was not difficult for a mostly African American jury to be suspicious of law enforcement when they were told that some of O. J. Simpson's blood was missing and one of the detectives was carrying the blood around with him. Although a White jury would reject any arguments of evidence tampering, a mostly African American jury would not be so quick to accept a White officer's declaration of no wrongdoing. African Americans know that law enforcement officers do wrong regularly.

Another consequence of police brutality is that innocent White citizens pay for the wrongdoing of White officers. Commonly, many African Americans see all or most Whites as being the same. While some African Americans may feel powerless to counter brutality by a White officer, they, given that they are motivated to commit crimes, do not have this sense of powerlessness when they see a potential White victim. In short, many times vulnerable Whites pay for the brutality of police officers. Although critics will often comment that a crime was senseless or unnecessarily brutal, it may be that the offender saw it, although wrong, as justice or payback. As an example, one African American young male was convicted of killing a White officer as the officer sat in his cruiser. This young man's father had been killed by a police officer years earlier when this African American was a little boy, and there likely was a connection between these two events. While one would not justify this type of response, one can understand that some events are connected.

Illustrating this connection, police officers are known to retaliate against some African Americans for the conduct of one African American. Innocent African Americans pay when a police officer is killed by an African American. Police brutality increases as these officers seek revenge. In Virginia, after the killing of two officers by a fifteen-year-old boy who contended that he was being brutalized in the police station and pulled an officer's gun and shot in self-defense, African Americans were increasingly stopped in this county, had shotguns pointed at them, were called niggers, and were urged to run so that the officers could kill them (Washington Afro-American, 1999). This response occurred although the teenager was in custody; these officers were angry and wanting to hurt other African Americans for what this boy had done. In New Orleans, police officers went on a killing spree one night in an African American community after one officer was killed. Several African Americans were killed as these officers sought revenge (Cooper & Cannizaro, 1993). There is no doubt that police officers engage in retaliation. Hence, just as these officers retaliate, some members in the African American community retaliate too against Whites.

Conclusion

Like White Americans, African Americans want crimes in their neighborhood to be prevented, and if not, solved and punished. However, African Americans do not want law enforcement treating everyone in the community as criminals and using Gestapo tactics. White Americans have crimes in their neighborhoods, but law enforcement does not use Gestapo tactics there. If a White man is identified as a suspect in the sexual molestation of children in a neighborhood, every White man in the neighborhood is not treated as a suspect. Further, if a White woman is acting bizarrely, she is not going to be shot. White people are not likely to be beaten for talking back to an officer. White mass murderers are not treated badly by law enforcement when they are apprehended. But an African American who has been suspected of minor theft might die during an arrest or be beaten severely. Although Attorney General Reno says that police brutality undermines community support by African Americans, I contend that the lack of punishment and the lack of justice is the real problem.

5

African Americans and the Military

A<small>FRICAN</small> A<small>MERICANS HAVE LONG</small> served in the military, dating from the colonial period to the Iraqi war in 2003 that overthrew Saddam Hussein. Their service to America has been marked consistently by discrimination and the lack of recognition. Very few movies made from the beginning of the film industry to the 1960s depicted the roles of African Americans in the military (Schubert, 2003). In the 1990s, movies were made about the Tuskegee Airmen from World War II and the African American Massachusetts Regiment in the Civil War made famous by the movie "Glory."

Skeptics might question any mistreatment of African American soldiers today, pointing out that during the Persian Gulf War in 1991 to remove the Iraqi army from Kuwait, the Commander in Chief who had headed the Joint Chiefs of Staff was General Colin Powell, an African American. Yet, in the Iraqi war that began in 2003, racial differences are seen in the differential treatment of Jessica Lynch, a White female soldier, and Shoshana Johnson, an African American female—both of whom were injured, taken prisoner, and subsequently freed. Jessica Lynch was quickly hailed as a heroine, lauded excessively in the White news media, and awarded a book and movie deal. Shoshana Johnson, however, was literally ignored, except for meeting with the Congressional Black Caucus, an appearance on BET (Black Entertainment Television), and marshalling a parade for Black cowboys. Shoshana Johnson's treatment is typical of how African Americans in the military have been slighted.

In 2003, Representative Charles Rangel, a member of the Congressional Black Caucus and a veteran of the Korean War, proposed a bill to reinstitute the draft. Representative Rangel's reasoning for advocating a return to the draft was twofold. First, he believed that politicians would be not as quick to advocate for war, as President Bush was doing prior to attacking Iraq, if the children of the rich and powerful were fighting the war. Second, closely tied to the first reason, was that minorities are most likely to fight and die. Representative Rangel's latter charge quickly prompted the Pentagon to release statistics on the percentage of African American soldiers killed in combat in Iraq and assert that African Americans were not dying in greater proportion to their numbers in the population or in the service. This second accusation, and its rebuttal, have been a concern of African Americans who believe that African Americans have died in greater numbers than what one would expect based on the Vietnam conflict. This chapter discusses the historical service of African Americans who served in the military as well as current issues.

African Americans' Participation in the Service during the Colonial Period

A seaman and former runaway slave, Crispus Attucks, was one of the first persons to be killed in the Boston Massacre on March 25, 1770, which was considered to be the first battle of the American Revolution (Lindenmeyer, 1970). About 5,000 African Americans served under George Washington out of a total of about 300,000 men under his command. African Americans fought in every major battle in the Revolutionary War (Lindenmeyer, 1970). African Americans served with the Swamp Fox, Francis Marion, in the Carolinas, and they also served in the Navy with John Paul Jones. Casear Tarrant, an African American, was the pilot for the *Patriot*, and under his command captured a British warship. Another African American, named Mark Starlin, served in the Navy as a captain and distinguished himself by making several raids on British ships. However, Starlin was later reclaimed by his owner and died a slave, although a statute existed that said that slaves who fought would be freed (Lindenmeyer, 1970).

During the Revolutionary War, some states permitted White men who were called to serve in the militia to send their slaves in their place to fight (Lindenmeyer, 1970). For example, Jack Arabas, a slave owned by Thomas Ivers, served in the Continental Army and was discharged from service. His owner, a New Yorker, wanted Arabas to return as his servant, but Arabas ran away to Connecticut. Ivers apprehended him and had put him in jail for safekeeping while he stayed in New Haven. Jack applied to a court for a writ of habeas corpus, contending that he was being held in jail illegally. Upon hearing Arabas' case, a judge freed Arabas, holding that Arabas' participation in the service entitled him to his freedom (*Jack Arabas v. Thomas Ivers*, 1784).

Southern states, while holding Africans in slavery, were not above using them in the militia to protect the states. In 1708, South Carolina passed a statute authorizing the assistance of slaves. It provided that in the case of invasion and for the safety of the province to have "the assistance of our trusty slaves, to serve us against our enemies . . . and that said slaves should be rewarded for the good service they may do us" (Statute at Large of South Carolina, 1708). The statute also provided that any slaveowner who refused to send his or her slaves during an invasion would be fined, and any slave who killed or captured one or more invaders, as attested by a White person, would be freed (Statute at Large of South Carolina, 1708). In Virginia, slaves were reported to have run away and joined the service. Thus, the Virginia legislature passed a law in 1777 that forbade military recruiters from signing up Africans unless the Africans could prove by Justices of the Peace that the Africans were free men (Hening's Virginia Statutes at Large, 1777).

During the War of 1812, African American sailors served on ships that fought the British. About 17 percent of these fighters were African Americans. On Lake Erie, Captain Oliver Hazard Perry won a victory against the British and under his command were four hundred sailors, with over one hundred of these men African Americans. Captain Perry's victory enabled General William Henry Harrison to cross Michigan and defeat the withdrawing British at the Battle of the Thames (Buckley & Bolden, 2003).

Similar to the Revolutionary War and the War of 1812, during the Civil War, Whites could have slaves sent to the military in their place. For example, a seventeen-year-old African American male named Cole was apprenticed to Gent, a White man, whose son had been drafted. Rather than send his son, the White man signed up his African American apprentice. Cole served in the army for fourteen months. Upon Cole's discharge, he learned that the pay for a substitute ranged from $300 to $900. Cole had a broker testify about a fair amount and the court awarded Cole $300. However, the Maryland appellate court reversed the judgment, holding that Cole had not suffered any damages and that the testimony of the substitute broker was improper (*Gent v. Cole*, 1873).

In a North Carolina case, Colonel Patton in the North Carolina line during the Revolutionary War enlisted his slave, Frederick, as a musician. Frederick died during the war and Colonel Patton later died too. The University of North Carolina was a trustee for Colonel Patton's estate. Under North Carolina law, a soldier who served his country was entitled to one thousand acres of land, and a North Carolina court assigned the one thousand acres to Frederick. The land was transferred several times to different owners, and a fight ensued in a Tennessee court over the one thousand acres. A key aspect of the case was whether a slave could acquire land. Citing the common law, the Tennessee court declared that what is earned by a slave belonged to the master.

When a slave, said the court, was enlisted in the army by his master, the master received the reward of his service—the bounty money and the pay (*University et al. v. Cambreling*, 1834).

The federal government in 1862 authorized President Lincoln to employ as many persons of African descent as he believed necessary to help put down the Southern rebellion (Federal Statute, 12 Statute 589). Many African Americans thus joined the Union army. About 180,000 African American soldiers served in the Union Army (Schubert, 2003). One African American named James Clark joined the army on August 11, 1863. On October 17, 1863, President Lincoln issued a proclamation calling on governors of several states to each raise 300,000 men, and Clark was counted as part of the quota for Maryland. The city of Baltimore had a pool of money to pay a bounty of $200 for every man who enlisted. Clark was honorably discharged on May 4, 1866 and applied for the $200 bounty. However, because he joined the army prior to President Lincoln's request, both a trial court and an appellate court ruled that he was not entitled to the bounty (*Clark v. Mayor*, 1868).

African Americans in the Military Post–Civil War

Following the Civil War, Congress also created exclusive African American troops who fought Native Americans, Mexicans, and the Spaniards. Congress, in 1866, created two African American cavalries—the Ninth and Tenth Cavalry; and four infantry regiments—the Thirty-eighth to the Forty-first. The Tenth Cavalry included Lieutenant Henry O. Flipper, the first African American graduate of West Point (Black & Black, 1985). African American soldiers became known as Buffalo Soldiers. This name was given to them by Native Americans. Native Americans called African American soldiers Buffalo Soldiers because African Americans' hair resembled the hair on the buffalo heads between the two horns (Schubert, 2003).

During the frontier period, there were about twenty-five thousand soldiers in the West, and the Buffalo Soldiers made up about three thousand men. They were in the West from 1866 to 1891 and participated in many campaigns against Native Americans. Eighteen Buffalo Soldiers received the Medal of Honor for bravery during various battles with Native Americans (Schubert, 2003).

These cavalries and infantry regiments constituted about 12,500 African American troops. As construction parties and railroad surveyors made their way West, African American soldiers provided escort and protection. African American soldiers fought Native Americans in Texas, New Mexico, Colorado, and Arizona. Some African Americans served as scouts for the army and one died at the Little Big Horn battle, where General Custer and his troops were massacred (Lindenmeyer, 1970).

As one historian noted, the scout, Isaiah Dorman, might have prevented the massacre if General Custer had sought Dorman's counsel. General Custer believed that his cavalry could easily defeat Indians and would not use Dorman. Dorman was a former slave who had escaped from his owner and lived with Native Americans. He married an Indian woman and the Sioux called Dorman the "Black White Man." The Indians trusted Dorman but the White officers lacked confidence in him and did not want to acknowledge that the Indians had legitimate grievances. Dorman was injured during the battle, and when told that Dorman was injured on the battlefield, Chief Sitting Bull, who led the fight against the soldiers, came to Dorman's side as Dorman lay dying. At that time, it was customary for Native Americans to scalp and mutilate soldiers' bodies because it was believed that they could not function in the afterlife without being whole or having an intact body. However, Chief Sitting Bull ordered that Dorman's body not be mutilated (Lindenmeyer, 1970).

In February 1898, Spain sank the U.S. battleship *Maine* in Havana Harbor. Among the dead were twenty-two African American sailors. America declared war on Spain and the battles were fought mostly in Cuba. African American troops were dispatched to Cuba along with White troops. Although Teddy Roosevelt and the Rough Riders received considerable accolades for charging up San Juan Hill, the Tenth Company, consisting of African Americans, was charging up the hill with Teddy and the Rough Riders, and their bravery was noted and recognized by the White soldiers.

African American soldiers also were used in the Philippines in 1898 and they were instrumental in putting down the rebellion there. In both campaigns, African American troops distinguished themselves, although they were sensitive to the fact that they were fighting dark-skinned Cubans and dark-skinned Filipinos yearning not to be dominated by America. At the same time, African American troops were incurring unappreciation and hostility from White America (Alt & Alt, 2002).

Violence against African American Soldiers: 1900s to World War II

One of the by-products of African Americans serving in the military was that they became convinced that they were as good as any White man and that they were not going back to being docile and subservient to white supremacy. The results of their defiance were that they were subject to unfair punishments, executions by hanging, and outright mob lynching. Sometimes, mob violence or arrests would be triggered by African American soldiers not adhering to Jim

Crow laws and sitting in the back of public transportation, not stepping aside when Whites walked down the street, or just having on a uniform. African Americans' service to the country in numerous past conflicts meant nothing to Whites.

For example, in 1906, African American soldiers representing the Twenty-fifth Infantry were ordered from Fort Niobrara, Nebraska, to Fort Brown, which was near Brownsville, Texas. The African American soldiers were to replace a White infantry. Immediately, the citizens of Brownsville protested to the War Department. Secretary of War William Howard Taft responded that there was universal prejudice throughout the country against African American soldiers, and African American soldiers were no more likely to create problems than White soldiers. Many of the citizens put up signs stating that they did not want "niggers" in their businesses. A rumor circulated that an African American soldier tried to rape a White woman. Then, some shootings happened and the African American soldiers were blamed (Foner, 1974).

The Army investigated and quickly concluded that some of the African American soldiers had done the shooting and that the other African American soldiers were protecting them with a wall of silence. The soldiers were told that if they did not inform on the guilty parties that all would be court-martialed. President Theodore Roosevelt ordered that the court-martials be carried out but not publicized until after the election. A week after the elections, 167 African American soldiers were court-martialed. One soldier had been in the army for twenty-seven years, and twenty-five of the soldiers had served more than ten years. All were discharged without honor, declared ineligible for pensions, and precluded from obtaining civil service employment. On September 28, 1972, the Army decided that the African American soldiers were denied justice and changed their discharge to honorable. However, the Army ruled that the survivors or their descendants were not entitled to back pay. One survivor, who was then eighty-six years old, was found in Minneapolis, and he reported that he had worked most of his life shining shoes and as a janitor. Congress then gave him $25,000 in compensation and permitted him to get medical care at a VA Hospital (Foner, 1974).

In 1917, African American soldiers stationed near Houston, Texas, had numerous problems with White citizens and police officers. On one occasion, an African American soldier was beaten by police officers because the soldier protested the beating of an African American woman by the police. When another highly respected African American soldier was beaten and jailed, some African American soldiers decided that they had had enough. They armed themselves and went to see about their jailed friend. They encountered police officers and a mob and shooting occurred. At the end of the shooting, sixteen Whites, including four police officers, were dead and four African American soldiers had died.

Two months later, sixty-four African Americans were court-martialed for murder and mutiny. In a very hasty trial, thirteen were sentenced to death, forty-two received life imprisonment, and five were acquitted. Within about two or three weeks, the thirteen condemned African American soldiers were hanged and did not have any review of their trials. The death sentences and hangings were kept secret until after the men had been executed. Later, twenty-eight more African American soldiers were tried, with sixteen soldiers receiving death sentences, and twelve sentenced to life imprisonment. Because of the outcry of the African American community and the NAACP, the president commuted ten of the sixteen death sentences to life imprisonment; the remaining six men were subsequently hanged. All in all, 118 African American soldiers were indicted and all were convicted except for 8 African American soldiers who testified in favor of the government in exchange for immunity. Because of the unfairness of the case, Congress passed a law that before a death sentence could be imposed on a soldier, the soldier was entitled to appellate review at the department level (Foner, 1974).

Other violent incidents that were mostly extralegal occurred after World War II. Walter White documented numerous lynchings of African American soldiers following World War II. In Walton County, Georgia, in 1946, an African American soldier who had just been honorably discharged from the Army objected to a White man's sexual advance to the African American's wife. They fought over this personal affront. The White man was sent to the hospital, and the African American was jailed for attacking him. Upon release from jail, taken to a secluded spot by deputies, the African American soldier, his wife, a male friend, and his friend's wife all were lynched (White, 1948). In Minden, Louisiana, an African American who had been honorably discharged from the army was accused of loitering in the backyard of a White woman and jailed with his seventeen-year-old cousin. The White woman refused to press charges and reports were that the charge was bogus. Friends of the soldier later stated that a White man had wanted a war souvenir that the soldier had, and the soldier refused to give his souvenir to the White man, incurring his wrath. The soldier and his cousin were told that the charges were groundless and they were free to go. The problem was that their "discharge" was late at night and they refused to leave the jail. The deputy forced them out of the jail and outside was a car with armed White men. The two African Americans were taken out and severely beaten. The soldier died but the young cousin survived (White, 1948).

Current Controversies: African Americans' Deaths from Conflicts, the Return of the Draft, and Jessica Lynch and Shoshana Johnson

One of the major controversies involving African Americans and the military occurred when African American Representative Charles Rangel, a veteran of the Korean War, introduced the Universal Service Act of 2003. At that time, he stated that the burden of sacrificing should be shared among all social classes. He then added that African Americans and the poor were serving in the armed services disproportionately to their numbers in the population.

Statistical data provided some support to the concerns of African Americans regarding the Vietnam conflict. Two years before the end of the Vietnam war, 5,570 African Americans had been killed, which constituted 23 percent of the men killed (Alt & Alt, 2002). At that time African Americans were 11 percent of the U.S. population (Alt & Alt, 2002). When the percentage of African American soldiers killed reached 25 percent, policy changes, due to criticisms, were made to lessen the number of African Americans on the front line (Alt & Alt, 2002).

When Representative Rangel made his accusation in 2003, he was quickly attacked as a racist and for playing the race card (Filbeck, 2003; Sparkman, 2003). The Pentagon quickly released statistical data to refute Representative Rangel's assertion. In releasing those statistics and offering counterarguments, the Pentagon conceded, indirectly, that African Americans' concerns regarding Vietnam were correct. Curtis L. Gilroy, a senior analyst for the Secretary of Defense, stated, "I would say that the perception that African Americans suffer more would be wrong today, *as opposed to years ago during the Vietnam War*" [emphasis by the author] (Fear, 2003, p. A03). Gilroy reported that African Americans now made up 21 percent of the military and many of them served in administration, combat support, and the medical fields. In 2000, the Defense Department reported that African Americans made up nearly 30 percent of the enlistees, and African American women made up nearly 50 percent of the women in the armed forces (Fear, 2003).

Another sore spot among African Americans was the differential treatment between Jessica Lynch and Shoshana Johnson. African Americans do not begrudge Jessica Lynch the attention and financial rewards that she has received but criticize the White media and the White public for ignoring Shoshana Johnson. African Americans talked about this issue among themselves and called in to radio shows to express the apparent racism there. As expected, Whites quickly disclaimed that racism had anything to do with the differences. On one television show, a White reporter asked his White guest to comment on African Americans' charge that racism was being exhibited in the differential treatment between Jessica Lynch and Shoshana Johnson. Conducting a comparison and contrast, this White guest stated that Shoshana Johnson did not want a book or movie deal and only wanted more disability. (Jessica Lynch was to receive 80 percent disability and Shoshana Johnson 30 percent.) Continuing, the White guest stated that Jessica Lynch was injured worse than Shoshana Johnson. Then, he added the coup de grâce, which was that Jessica

Lynch had blond hair and blue eyes. The White reporter said nothing about the obvious racism in that statement, as well as the previous statement that Johnson only wanted more disability. In trying to refute racism, both the reporter and the guest confirmed racism.

The saga of Jessica Lynch also reveals subtle racism in that it showed how White heroes are sometimes created. After Jessica Lynch was captured and members of her unit were killed, the Pentagon released a story that "she went down fighting and had fired her weapon until she was out of ammunition." The White news media, especially the White female reporters, proudly and incessantly told the public how brave this young White woman had been. Later, when she was released, to her credit, Jessica Lynch stated that this story about her firing her weapon until it was empty was not true. Jessica Lynch never fired her weapon because it jammed (Starr, 2003). Interestingly, not one reporter criticized the Pentagon for releasing this false story in an attempt to create a White female heroine.

Given that the Pentagon decided to lie, why did the Pentagon not lie for the African American woman? Why could not the African American woman have gone down fighting? Jessica Lynch represents a pattern of highlighting White achievements, whether true or false, and ignoring African Americans. Teddy Roosevelt became a household name when he was shown to have charged up San Juan Hill, but few history books and newspaper drawings show pictures of the Buffalo Soldiers going up San Juan Hill too, alongside Teddy Roosevelt and his Rough Riders.

Reflections and Analyses of African Americans in the Military Presently

Representative Charles Rangel was quickly criticized for stating prior to the commencement of the Iraqi War that African Americans and the poor would die disproportionately to Whites. Statistics were quickly presented showing comparisons of deaths in combat of Whites and African Americans. While Whites are indeed more likely to die in combat, the data show that more African Americans have died in various wars than any other minority. For instance, Latinos are now the largest minority group in this country, and they have long been a significant force in this country in terms of numbers (Population Resource Center, 2004).

As an illustration, 3,075 African Americans died in the Korean War, compared to 306 Hispanics and 575 Mixed Race Hispanics, 148 Hawaiians, 104 Native Americans or Alaska Natives, and 241 Asians (Department of Defense, 2004). (The author is using the ethnic designations from the Pentagon because it identified Hispanics and Mixed Race Hispanics rather than the preferred designation of Latinos.) For the Vietnam War, 7,241 African Americans died, compared to 349 Mixed Race Hispanics, 229 Hawaiians, 226 Native Americans or Alaska Natives, and 139 Asians. During the Persian Gulf War, 63 African Americans died, 1 Hispanic and 14 Mixed Race Hispanics, 2 Hawaiians, 3 Native Americans or Alaska Natives, and 1 Asian (Department of Defense, 2004).

The Department of Defense also released the death data from 1980 to March 15, 2003. According to these data, 5,998 African Americans died, 366 Hispanics and 322 Mixed Race Hispanics died, 120 Hawaiians died, 151 Native Americans died, and 332 Asians died (Department of Defense, 2004).

African Americans have long viewed the military as a place that provided more opportunities than they could find in the general public. However, problems have long occurred in the military, beginning with the colonial wars, up to present times. In the 1950s, an African American Marine wrote to the president of the United States requesting that his citizenship be forfeited and that he be allowed to move to a foreign country so that his family would not starve. In the 1970s, racial problems emerged in some branches of the military and the military instituted various kinds of training to combat conflict between White servicemen and African American servicemen. Representative Ronald V. Dellums, a member of the Congressional Black Caucus, requested that the U.S. General Accounting Office provide information on racial discrimination in the military. In response to Representative Dellums' request, a report was generated that reviewed seventy-two studies on various aspects of discrimination in the military. This report showed that African Americans were overrepresented in court-martials, African Americans had the least positive perceptions of equal opportunity in the military, and African Americans were the most underpromoted group compared to other minority groups (General Accounting Office, 1995).

Returning to Jessica Lynch, she continues to be used as a White symbol. A full-page advertisement appeared in the *Columbus Dispatch* on May 2, 2004, involving a program called "Get Motivated." It was a seminar that was held at Nationwide Arena, which holds about 24,000 people. Five speakers provided various lectures and one of the speakers was Jessica Lynch. Her presentation was entitled "Survival Is a Choice" and the advertisement stated that "Private Jessica Lynch astonished the world when she survived the unthinkable and was rescued from Iraqi capture. You will be amazed as she shares the key strategies that she used to survive and thrive in the most brutal of circumstances" (*Columbus Dispatch*, May 2, 2004, p. E16). She is listed as providing information on:

1. How to Win Against All Odds
2. Developing the Discipline of a Survivor

3. How to Eliminate Fear and Amplify Confidence
4. Resolving Crisis: 3 Tactics that Get Results
5. How You Can Solve Impossible Problems.

This seminar provided paid employment for Jessica Lynch. It also reflects poorly on the two other minority women who were with Jessica Lynch—Shoshana Johnson and Lori Piestewa, a Native American woman who was killed. Shoshana Johnson was shot and Piestewa died after her vehicle was hit with a Rocket Propelled Grenade (RPG) and the vehicle crashed. Piestewa's wounds were mortal. Piestewa did not die because she chose NOT to survive, but because her wounds were very serious. The clear implication of Jessica Lynch's presentation was that some soldiers choose not to survive, which is not the case. Simply, Jessica Lynch was luckier than Lori Piestewa.

Conclusion

While African Americans have complained about the military through the years, their complaints have not and do not indicate that they were or are unpatriotic or do not love this country. As the data show, African Americans die more than any other minority group. Also, in the present voluntary armed services, they are more likely to enlist than any other minority group. Arguably, they are more likely to enlist in the armed services because of a lack of equal opportunity in society. Moreover, African Americans know that armed service might be a stepping-stone to the middle class, providing not only some advancement opportunities in the service but also educational benefits and homeownership later. African Americans tend to view the armed services as less discriminatory as a whole, at least until they actually enlist into one of the branches.

African Americans complain about discrimination in society and the military, but they have served from the colonial period for no pay and no recognition and are presently in the military in greater numbers than all other minority groups. As Shoshana Johnson has shown, recognition remains difficult, and this lack of recognition is a lack of justice.

6

African Americans and Economic Discrimination

AFRICAN AMERICANS HAVE LESS wealth than almost any racial group in America (Keister, 2000). Conservatives suggest that the reasons for African Americans having less wealth and social resources are that African Americans are less industrious and more likely to rely on government programs (Murray, 1984). One social scientist, as a result of her research, said that African Americans are less inclined to engage in businesses that produce wealth. Frequently, African Americans' critics point to a newly arrived group and point to their financial successes. Keister (2000) has conducted considerable research on the relationship between race and wealth accumulation. Among her other variables were earnings, education, marital behavior, and fertility. She found that Whites are more likely to seek high-risk and high-return opportunities and that racial differences in education account for Whites having more wealth. Keister's data and analysis fail to consider the historical effects and aftermaths involving African Americans and economics.

Whites have long viewed African Americans as economic commodities to be exploited. Writing the preface for a book on how the poor are exploited, U.S. Representative Maxine Waters stated that banks, savings and loan institutions, insurance companies, and mortgage companies have steadfastly redlined, discriminated against, and disinvested in poor neighborhoods and communities of color (Hudson, 1996). Even when poor people have their tax returns completed, they are, as one national community organization charged, exploited by tax preparers and lending institutions. An organized national protest was held to protest H & R Block's instant refund program, which is actually called a refund anticipation loan and is in fact loans provided

by a lending institution for a fee. After a person's taxes are completed and a refund is anticipated, the poor person may get his or her money that day. The
interest and fees are deducted from the refund, and the refund check goes to
the lending institution. The interest and fees charged for getting a loan more
than doubles the cost for preparing poor people's taxes, earning one refund
anticipation lender $1.14 billion in 2003 (Williams, 2004).

However, these exploitative practices have their roots in African Americans'
experiences with slavery and following slavery. Beginning with slavery,
Africans were viewed as property, and owners could leave slaves to their heirs
like cattle, land, money, and houses (Craig-Taylor, 2000). Insurance policies
were sold to slaveowners to protect slaveowners from losses, and slaves were
used as collateral for loans (Cox, 2002). In short, enslaved Africans increased
the wealth of slaveowners, which is a form of economic discrimination when
viewed from the perspectives of slaves.

After slavery, other forms of economic discrimination emerged. Numerous
studies have found that the lynching of African Americans had a strong cor-
relation with economic conditions and economic competition by African
Americans (Beck & Tolnay, 1995; Soule, 1992; Tolnay, Beck, & Massey, 1992).
In other words, when the price of cotton went down, more lynching of African
Americans occurred (Beck & Tolnay, 1990), and when the population of
African American workers increased, more lynching occurred (Corzine, Huff-
Corzine, & Creech, 1988). Numerous reports exist that show that as newly
freed slaves increased their political and economic statuses, Whites would become uncomfortable and set out to destroy nascent African American communities (DeLatte, 1994; Formwalt, 1994; Hennessey, 1994). Such attacks led
to countless African Americans being killed and their communities being
burned to the ground.

For example, Lovett (1994) wrote about the racial climate in Memphis, Tennessee, in 1865 and 1866. Whites resented and feared African Americans' "expansion of independent black economics because black hack drivers, teamsters, skilled craftsmen, and ordinary laborers were already depriving whites
of jobs" (p. 210). As one White woman wrote, "one good result of the Memphis Riot and massacres was the improved behavior of the Negroes. Even the
Negroes next door to us at No. 95 Union Street moved away to less respectable
quarters" (Lovett, 1994, p. 226).

The most serious violence occurred in Colfax Parish, Louisiana, in 1873,
when more than two hundred African Americans were killed (Tolnay & Beck,
1995). Following the massacre, one White man said, "a nigger in that parish
puts his hat under his arm now when he talks to a white man. They are the
most respective things you ever saw. But before the fight, oh, Lord? There was
no living with them" (Tolnay & Beck, 1995, p. 6). Yet, there was no fight. The

aim of this violence was to prevent African Americans from acquiring land, getting an education, and entering politics and to ensure that "southern whites were to continue to enjoy an economy in which blacks labored to create wealth for the privileged" (Tolnay & Beck, 1995, p. 5).

Another form of economic discrimination was the creation of restrictive racial covenants that forbade Whites from selling or renting property, mostly houses, to persons of African descent. The effect of this discrimination was not only to prevent African Americans from elevating their social and economic statuses but to restrict them to the worst areas of cities. These racially exclusive covenants were not held to be illegal until the late 1940s by the U.S. Supreme Court. Then, the Court ruled that it was not illegal for private persons to enter into these contracts, but how they were enforced was illegal. Economic discrimination, however, still occurred—often transforming into different forms and shapes.

Now, in 2004 economic discrimination still occurs. As before, African Americans are viewed as people to be exploited by White businesses. Several lawsuits have been filed against companies that discriminate by charging African Americans and Latinos, more than similarly comparable Whites, higher interest rates for car loans. Also, redlining (i.e., the practice of starving an area of capital simply because minorities live in those areas) by insurance companies and lending institutions continues to be identified as a problem. This chapter more fully discusses these critical issues.

Discrimination in the Acquisition of
Real Property: Racially Restricted Covenants

Historically, widespread discrimination, supported by state and federal legal systems, existed in preventing African Americans from acquiring real property on a national scale. Many of these agreements specified descendents of Africans, Ethiopians, Negroes, or Mongolians. One covenant signed in St. Louis, Missouri, required all property owners to sign an agreement that "no part of said property or any portion thereof shall be, for said term of fifty-years, occupied by any person not of the Caucasian race, it being intended hereby to restrict the use of said property for said period of time again the occupancy as owners of tenants of any portion of said property for resident or other purpose by people of the Negro or Mongolian Race" (*Shelley et ux. v. Kraemer et ux.,* 1948, p. 838). Another covenant in West Virginia forbade sales to any Ethiopians. In this case, a White couple sold a lot to African Americans, and the owner of a neighboring plot of land sued the seller. A lower court forbade the sale of the land to the African American couple and ordered the African American couple not to take title to the land. Although this decision was reversed, the focus was on the right of a White person to sell his land and legal problems with the language in the deed restriction (*H. B. White v. Lewis White*, 1929).

In Addesleigh, a reserved section of St. Albans, Queens County, New York, a group of homeowners executed a covenant and agreed that they would sell their property to White people or Caucasians only. The only African Americans allowed in the homes were employees or maids. One couple, after signing the agreement, decided later to sell their home to an African American couple. The other owners sued in court to stop it. The New York appellate court rejected the defense that the New York and U.S. Constitutions forbade racial discrimination in that matter. The court noted that the Fourteenth Amendment was a prohibition against the state and had no restraint on private persons' decisions and agreement to discriminate. Thus, the court ruled against the couple that tried to sell their home to the African American couple (*Dury et al. v. Neely et ux.*, 1942).

An Ohio appellate court ruled that a restriction in a deed against the use or occupancy of land to non-Caucasians was valid and enforceable. The agreement among owners of twenty-nine lots in downtown Columbus, Ohio, agreed that no one would lease, rent, or sell a lot to any person or persons of any race other than Caucasians and no person other than a Caucasian would be permitted to occupy premises, except as a servant of the occupants (*Perkins v. Trustees of Monroe Avenue Church of Christ*, 1946). In North Carolina, an appellate court held that a deed with a covenant that the land could not be sold or occupied by anyone of the Negro race was legally enforceable (*D. L. Phillips and Wife, Louise E. Phillips v. R. M. Wearn*, 1946).

In Detroit, Michigan, the Northwest Civil Association sued an African American male to prevent him from moving into a home. Reportedly, a home was sold to a married woman who claimed that her husband traveled a lot. She was accompanied to the sale by her parents. The woman and her parents all looked White and the salesperson testified that he thought that the woman was White and assumed that her husband was White too. The agent selling the home testified that he was deceived and that the woman and her parents knew that a Negro was forbidden from moving into the subdivision because this was a selling point that he used. The agent told the court that he always told homebuyers that the subdivision was for Whites only and that no Negroes would ever be allowed to buy a home in the subdivision. Accordingly, the trial court and the appellate court ordered the defendant, Otis E. Sheldon, not to use or occupy the home and declared that he had ninety days to vacate the home (*Northwest Civil Association v. Shelton*, 1947).

The U.S. Supreme Court initially sanctioned these rulings and provided guidance for lower federal courts and states' supreme courts. In *Corrigan et al.*

v. Buckley (1926), the Court held that it lacked jurisdiction to hear a case from the court of appeals and ruled that racially restrictive covenants did not violate any amendments to the U.S. Constitution. In this case, several Whites sued to prevent the sale of a lot to an African American. The covenant prohibited "the use and occupancy by negroes [*sic*] of the various premises covered by its terms, but it also prevents the sale, conveyance, lease or gift of any such premises by any of the owners or their heirs and assigns to negroes [*sic*] or to any person or persons of the negro [*sic*] race or blood, perpetually, or at least for a period of twenty-one years" (*Corrigan et al. v. Buckley*, 1926, pp. 325–326). The White plaintiffs won in the U.S. district court and in the court of appeals.

In 1948, the U.S. Supreme Court held that racially restricted covenants violated the rights of African Americans. The Court decided two cases—one from Michigan and one from Missouri. The Michigan covenant forbade the sale of property to any Negro or members of the Mongolian race for fifty years and the Missouri covenant forbade the occupation of property by any person or persons except those of the Caucasian race. The Court stated that restrictive agreements standing alone did not violate the constitutional rights of African Americans. The Court has held repeatedly that the Fourteenth Amendment prohibited state action as it clearly says that no *State* shall deprive any citizen of the right to life, liberty, or property without due process of law nor deny any person the equal protection of the law. Therefore, discrimination by private citizens did not implicate the Fourteenth Amendment. However, when state courts enjoined or forbade African Americans from acquiring property, occupying property, or leaving property, the courts' actions or orders constituted state action. As such, state courts were complicit in denying African Americans their rights to liberty, property, and equal protection of the laws (*Shelley et ux. v. Kraemer et ux.*, 1948).

States have been notorious in continuing racial practices after a court ruling. As an illustration, states were reluctant to end segregation in schools following the *Brown v. Board of Education* decision in 1954. Racial covenants might have been ruled illegal in 1948, but they certainly continued in practice. The damaging effects of racial covenants, as well as other housing discrimination issues, will be discussed later in the conclusion.

African Americans and the Taking of Property

Although African Americans had a difficult time acquiring housing property because of racial covenants, they were able to acquire some land, mostly in the South. This was so because of the limited protection of the federal government during the Reconstruction period following slavery (Craig-Taylor,

2000). The government had promised newly freed slaves forty acres of land and a mule, which most did not get. Some African Americans, however, were able in the South to run for office and acquire property and land like White immigrants. However, when the Reconstruction period ended, African Americans were driven from political offices by violence and concerted efforts emerged to destroy successful African Americans and take away their land by any means necessary. Two strategies were employed to drive African Americans from their land—violence and the law.

In 2001, the Associated Press printed a three-part investigative story—called *Torn from the Land*—in which it documented how land was taken from African Americans. The Associated Press interviewed over one thousand individuals and searched tens of thousands of public documents (Lewan & Barclay, 2001). They were able to confirm 107 land takings in thirteen southern and border states (Lewan & Barclay, 2001).

In 1910, African Americans owned 15 million acres of land, but in 2001 they owned 1.1 million acres (Lewan & Barclay, 2001). African Americans did not just sell the land and move away. More times than not, they were driven from the land by violence, as the Associated Press documented, and the law and legal systems were complicit in these land grabs.

Historians have stated that one of the prime reasons for targeting African Americans was to prevent African Americans from acquiring wealth. As reported by Dolores Barclay, Todd Lewan, and Allen G. Breed (2001), Paula J. Giddings, a Duke University historian, stated that "by the 1880s and 1890s, a significant number of blacks began to do well in terms of entrepreneurship and landownership and it simply couldn't be tolerated" (p. 4).

For example, in 1885 three African Americans opened the Peoples' Grocery Store in a rather large African American neighborhood in Memphis, Tennessee. A White man had a competing store across the street. Using a petty dispute between two boys in front of the Peoples' Grocery Store, one White man claimed that the storeowners were causing trouble. Nine deputy sheriffs in plain clothes and allegedly with arrest warrants went to the three African Americans at night to serve the warrants. Fearing that these men were part of a White mob, the three African American owners fired on the men, wounding some of them. They were arrested, but they were later taken from the jail by a White mob and their store was looted. The contents of the store were liquidated and the store was acquired by a deputy sheriff (Barclay, Lewan & Breed, 2001).

On September 10, 1932, fifteen Whites set fire to the courthouse in Paulding, Mississippi, where property records were held for the eastern half of the county where most African Americans lived. The next day, a dispute existed over who owned the eastern half and African Americans had no accepted proof of their land ownership (Lewan & Barclay, 2001). As a result, they lost their lands.

Violent Land Taking

Robert Gleed, a seventeen-year-old slave, ran away from his Virginia owner and took up residence in Columbus, Mississippi. Following the Civil War, he was able to acquire 295 acres of farmland, three city lots, a general store, and a nice home. Gleed was a prominent member of his community—president of the Mercantile Land and Banking Company, head of the County Chamber of Commerce, and a former state senator. He decided to run for Sheriff of Lowndes County. At that time, the county in which Columbus was located, Lowndes County, had 3,800 registered African American voters compared to 1,250 White registered voters. On November 1, 1875, Gleed lost everything. The day before the election, a White mob attacked Gleed supporters and burned Gleed's home. The mob threatened to kill Gleed and Gleed fled to Texas. A White man was then elected Sheriff.

Soon thereafter, two White persons claimed that Gleed owned them money and foreclosed on all his property. One Toby W. Johnston liquidated the store for $941 and kept the proceeds. One Bernard G. Hendrick, claiming that Gleed owned him $125, took 215 acres of land and purchased Gleed's home and an adjacent lot at auction for $11, and the remainder of Gleed's property was sold for $500. In the 1940s, Gleed's farm was sold to the federal government and one of Gleed's lots held four houses, a gas station, and a realty company. The president of the realty company, when told the history of the land, said that he did not care who owned the land previously, and that it sounded as if Gleed had abandoned his property (Lewan, 2001a).

Anthony P. Crawford, an African American, was one of the most prosperous farmers in Abbeville County, South Carolina, which was a status that infuriated Whites. While waiting to take his cotton to the gin mill in 1916, Crawford went into the store owned by W. D. Barksdale. Barksdale offered Crawford eighty-five cents a pound for his cottonseed, but Crawford declined, saying that he had a better offer. Barksdale called Crawford a liar, and Crawford called Barksdale a cheat. Three White employees grabbed ax handles to attack Crawford, who backed out of the store into the street. The sheriff appeared and arrested Crawford for cursing a White man. After making bail, Crawford was attacked by a mob and stabbed. The Sheriff rearrested Crawford and took him back to jail. Later, the sheriff gave the mob the key to Crawford's cell. Crawford was then taken out of town and lynched. Two Whites were appointed executors of Crawford's estate—including 427 areas of prime cotton land. One of the executors was Andrew J. Ferguson, who was related to one of the leaders of the mob. Ferguson sold the property, giving Crawford's children $200 each and keeping over $5,400 for himself. The cotton went to Barksdale. The Crawford family maintained the farm, which was valued at $20,000, for a while. But when they could not repay a loan, the farm was sold at auction for $504 (Barclay, Lewan & Breed, 2001).

Coercive Land Taking

On Sapelo Island, Georgia, in the 1950s, a rich and powerful White man who owned less-than-desirable sections of the island decided that he wanted the other, more desirable land on the island, owned by African Americans who had been on the island since the end of slavery. The White man was Richard J. Reynolds, Jr., the son of the builder of the biggest tobacco company in the United States. Reynolds' land was in Hog Hammock and the African Americans' land was in Raccoon Bluff. Reynolds was the only employer on Sapelo Island and owned the ferry from the island to the mainland. Reynolds decided that he wanted to swap his land, which was near a swampy enclave, with the more desirable and valuable land held by African Americans. One African American owner swapped her sixteen-acre tract on Raccoon Bluff for five and a half acres of Hog Hammock. An African American couple swapped nine acres on Raccoon Bluff for two acres of Hog Hammock. One other African American swapped four acres for two acres on Hog Hammock. Sometimes, the deed swap involved other considerations for African Americans. One African American reported that he was supposed to get some lumber too from Reynolds' lumber mill. But when the lumber came, he was forced to pay for it. More than a dozen African Americans made these land swaps and none turned down these swaps. When asked later why they did not reject these swaps, they reported that they could not because Reynolds owned everything. Sometimes, the person approaching them was the sheriff of the county, and he would insinuate that if they did not swap their land, then they would not have jobs. (The use of the sheriff also probably suggested to these families that they would find themselves in trouble with the law if they did not exchange their land.) When Reynolds died, his wife sold the land to the State of Georgia for $835,000 in 1969. Contacted in her home in Switzerland and asked if the land swaps were fair, she replied that she believed so and that her ex-husband had tried to do a good thing for the former African American landowners (Barclay, 2001a).

"Legal" Land Taking

Sometimes, land was taken from African Americans through legal means. For instance, a White car and farm equipment dealer in Lexington, Mississippi, Norman Weathersby, acquired considerable amounts of land from African American farmers in the 1950s and 1960s. He would sell used pickup trucks and used farm equipment in exchange for the borrowers' land as collateral. The trucks and farm equipment were in poor condition and would be in need of repairs shortly after borrowers acquired them. When African Americans missed one payment, Weathersby foreclosed. When Weathersby died in 1973, he left more than seven hundred acres of land that he had acquired from African Americans in these foreclosures (Barclay, 2001b).

Turf Smith, an African American living in Mississippi, lived on a 158-acre estate, along with about twenty-five family members spread out on the estate. He wanted to build a house on 2 acres, but could not get the other relatives to agree. Hearing of Smith's predicament, a lawyer offered to help him. However, the lawyer started a process that led to all the land being put up for auction, and at auction, a White man purchased 156 acres (Lewan, 2001).

The process in which Turf Smith lost his land is called partitioning—a legal maneuver available in all states involving land. Partitioning is a legal process that was initially designed to settle land ownership among heirs. However, normally the court is asked to partition the land, and by law, the partitioning must be done fairly. Land cannot be simply divided up, because some portions of land are more valuable than other portions; some land might have timber on it or is near a desirable location. So, rather than trying to divide land equally, the court simply orders that the land be put up for auction and the proceeds divided among the owners.

This problem typically occurs when a person dies without a will. A landowner who dies without a will causes the land to be jointly owned by all the heirs. The heirs do not own specific portions but they are viewed as joint owners. If others die without wills, the situation can become very complex. Anyone can purchase a share of the ownership of the land, however small. So, some Whites, finding an African American heir who is desperate and/or angry with the family, buy ownership in the land. Partitioning permits any owner to go to court and force the sale of the land. So, if there are fifty heirs/owners with forty-nine African Americans and one White man, the White man can force the land to be auctioned off even if the forty-nine others do not want to sell. All expenses, including legal expenses, in selling the land are taken off the top.

As an illustration, Louis Marsh, a freed slave, acquired 560 acres of land in Jackson Parish, Louisiana. Marsh died without a will in 1906, leaving the land to his children. There were seven children—one son, Kern Marsh, left Louisiana because of trouble with the criminal justice system. So, the judge gave the six remaining children 80 acres and gave them joint ownership of Kern Marsh's 80 acres. Albert Marsh farmed his 80 areas and the other siblings gave him permission to farm Kern Marsh's acres. Albert Marsh died without a will, and a White oilman, J. B. Holstead, purchased 11.4 acres from Albert Marsh's nephew, Leon Elmore, in 1955. Holstead gave Leon Elmore $100 and a used truck. The judge forced the sale of the 80 acres of land that was supposed to have gone to Kern Marsh. The judge ruled that the true owners of the 80 acres were not Kern Marsh's brothers and sisters, but Kern Marsh's heirs, which included Leon Elmore. Holstead asked the court for a court order to force the sale of the land with court costs, with Holstead's attorney fees to come from the proceeds from the sale. The judge granted Holstead's request on November 15, 1955, and Holstead purchased the 80 acres at auction for $6,400. Holstead then sold the land and the oil and gas rights for an unspecified amount. Holstead's son, a Houston attorney, when told of his father's land dealing stated that his father followed Louisiana's laws (Barclay & Lewan, 2001).

In South Carolina, Audrey Moffitt, a white real estate trader, sought 335 acres of land in 1990 that had been owned by the Becketts since 1873. There were seventy-six Beckett heirs and Moffitt went after the more elderly members. One Beckett was seventy-three years old and had cancer. Moffitt bought her one-seventy-sixth share for $750. The land was worth $4,653. Moffitt purchased other shares from elderly Becketts for $5,800, but these shares were worth $55,833. Moffitt filed a petition action in 1991 and she and another White real estate broker bought the land. Moffitt broke up her holdings and sold the land in pieces. She made $1,708,117 from her dealings with the Becketts' land. Another side of the Beckett clan who owned 50 acres of land came into contact with Moffitt, who purchased a share of it. Knowing of what Moffitt had done to their other relatives, they offered her the pick of any 10.4 acres if she would drop her petition process. Moffitt had paid $2,775 for the 10 acres of land and sold a roadway easement for $17,000 and the remaining land to a church for $200,000. Moffitt claimed that her dealings with the Becketts were fair and that the Becketts were to blame for having their lands in a mess (Barclay & Lewan, 2001).

Discrimination in Mortgage Lending

Homeownership was a dream to the average person and banks were reluctant to make loans for home buying. Banks' reluctance to make loans was especially strong in the 1930s during the height of the Depression. Then, banks required 50 percent down with the loan paid off in 5 to 7 years. The interest rate was due at the end of the loan in one lump payment, forcing the borrowers to take out another loan to make the final payment. The initial loan was from 6 to 8 percent and the second mortgage would be for 18 percent. In order to help the economy and to give unemployed homebuilders work, President Franklin Roosevelt created the Federal Home Administration (FHA). The FHA made homeownership possible by guaranteeing mortgages, requiring the borrowers to make a down payment of 10 percent, and extending payment over 30 years—the contemporary mortgage that we have today. Veterans under the G.I. Bill could get loans with no down payments.

Because the federal government was guaranteeing mortgages, the federal government did not want to make these highly desirable terms available for all property in the United States. Thus, the federal government sought to evaluate all property so that banks would know what type of property merited a federally backed loan. This enormous task of classifying property fell to a newly created agency in 1936—the Home Owner's Loan Corporation (HOLC). HOLC established strict standards. A surveyor looked for any sign of neighborhood decay or neglect that showed that a neighborhood was in decline. The surveyor would look for any sign of minorities in the neighborhood. Although foreign-born Whites and Jews were included as minorities, the surveyor generally looked for African Americans. Even one African American in a neighborhood would disqualify the entire neighborhood from getting any federally backed loans. After a year of surveying, the entire country had been divided into zones based on the characteristics of each neighborhood. Maps were developed to aid banks in making loans and these maps were highly confidential, with only federal officials and senior bankers allowed to see them. These officials would not acknowledge that these maps existed (Case, 2000).

To readily aid banks and restrict the loans, federal officials developed a grading and color system from A to D, with A being first-grade neighborhoods. The A areas were colored as green and had the full blessing of the federal government. Borrowers in the A areas had no African Americans, and banks were instructed to offer A borrowers the maximum amount of financing and the best terms. The next grade was B and these areas were colored in blue. These were good neighborhoods, but they were beginning to show some fray. Mortgage lenders were advised to make loans at 10 to 15 percent below the maximum. The next grade, C, was colored yellow. These were older neighborhoods with a declining style. Last, the bottom grade was D and it was colored red. The term redlining comes from this designation. D neighborhoods were struggling and deemed a losing struggle. These were the neighborhoods with ethnic minorities and banks were encouraged and supported in not making loans in these neighborhoods (Case, 2000).

Although the federal government and lending institutions created the practice of redlining, the federal government in subsequent years passed legislation outlawing racial discrimination in the housing market. For example, Congress passed the Fair Housing Act in 1968 and amended it in 1988. Congress also passed the Civil Rights Act of 1968, which had implications for fair housing, and the Equal Credit Opportunity Act. Yet, the practice was ingrained in banks, and many banks or lending institutions simply continued the practice of discrimination. Banks were also aided by insurance companies.

Discrimination in Insurance

Squires (2003) reported that there was much insidious racial profiling occurring in the insurance industry. Although banks have been accused of redlining or refusing to make loans in certain areas of a city, a more responsible industry is the insurance industry. Without insurance, banks do not loan and without loans, some individuals will not be able to acquire property, such as homes or commercial property. In the insurance industry, profiling "refers to practices through which individuals are classified, at least in part, on the basis of their race or the racial composition of their neighborhoods and treated differently as a result" (Squires, 2003, p. 394).

Insurance companies receive premiums from customers, which generally are paid at the beginning of the policy. They have no real idea whether they are charging enough for the policies because they do not know if a customer will have a loss and file a claim. Some individuals, such as homeowners, will pay their premiums and have no losses during the time that they are covered. Some individuals will pay their premiums and have losses that would exceed tremendously what they paid in premiums. So, the industry tries to predict who will have losses and who will not. Because it cannot collect data on each applicant for insurance because of the expense, it categorizes applicants by groups and the expected loss from each group (Squires, 2003). Insurance companies analyze two general types of hazards in their field—moral hazards and morale hazards.

Moral hazards are those hazards that might lead to fraud and morale hazards are those hazards that come from carelessness, knowing that a property is insured. On the surface, these might seem like sound business judgments, but they are not. Racial stereotyping permeates these decisions. One insurance agent in the 1950s remarked about the difficulty in assessing "acceptable and unacceptable colored or cheap mixed white areas" (Squires, 2003, p. 397).

While one might think that the 1950s may have been characterized by more racism and racial discrimination than contemporary times, in the 1990s, Nationwide Insurance had marketing materials that referred to "Low Income Southern Blacks" and "Urban Hispanics." When confronted and criticized for these labels, it changed them to "Hard Times" (Squires, 2003). But whatever the change, insiders would still know that the new label is a proxy for the old label. Other codes have been used to mask racial discrimination. For example, in 2002, one insurance agent asked whether a location had any Section 8 housing and whether the neighbor kids were more likely to play hockey or basketball (Squires, 2003). Clearly, Section 8 housing and basketball are code words for African Americans.

Although race is a factor in making decisions regarding who should be insured and who should not, racism may be counterproductive based on other statistics. For example, insurance companies consider moral hazards and whether an insured person is more likely to commit insurance fraud. According to the Bureau of Justice Statistics (1999), 68 percent of the individuals in federal prisons in 1998 for fraudulent property offenses were White compared to 28 percent being African Americans. Whites make up the majority of persons in prison for fraud, and some of these offenses are insurance fraud, as insurance fraud is a federal offense. The data were not available to show the different types of fraud, and the percentage of each racial group who had insurance and committed insurance fraud would be more informative; but one can surmise that Whites are more likely to commit insurance fraud. As a result, it does not make sense to deny African Americans insurance based on their moral hazards.

In 1988, the *Atlanta Journal Constitution* published a series entitled the "Color of Money," in which it detailed seemingly racial discrimination in lending institutions in the Fulton County, Georgia, area. The series earned the newspaper a Pulitzer Prize. Drawing the attention of the U.S. Department of Justice, the story led to an investigation and a historical lawsuit against the most egregious institution, Decatur Federal Savings and Loan Association (Ritter, 1996). In business since 1927, Decatur Federal was accused by the federal government of opening its branches primarily in White areas, advertising in White newspapers, avoiding originating loans from the Federal Housing Administration and the Veterans Administration, which tend to have African Americans' participation, employing few African Americans in key mortgage loan positions, and helping Whites to rewrite their loan applications while denying African Americans such assistance. The federal government also charged that "Decatur Federal rejected qualified black applicants more often than qualified white applicants, even after controlling for all relevant underwriting variables, such as income, credit history, net worth, debt ratios, employment history, and education level" (Goering & Wienk, 1996, p. 429).

As expected, Decatur Federal denied that it has engaged in discrimination, but it entered into a consent decree to avoid protracted litigation. Decatur Federal agreed to give one million dollars to 48 African Americans who were denied mortgages from 1988 to 1992. In addition, it agreed to advertise in African American news media, to open a branch office in an African American area, to provide pay incentives for executives who solicit business from the African American community, and to meet the needs of low and moderate income neighborhoods (Goering & Wienk, 1996).

Discrimination in Automobile Lending

In 1998, African Americans filed a lawsuit against General Motors Acceptance Corporation (GMAC) and Nissan Motor Acceptance Corporation (NMAC) accusing both corporations of racial discrimination in lending practices (Mayer, 2003). When a person buys a car, a loan application is completed and submitted to a lending institution. The interest rate is based on the borrower's creditworthiness, the amount and length of the loan, and the type of car, with a used car bringing a higher interest rate than a new car. Lenders then give dealers the flexibility to increase the rate, with the dealer keeping about 75 percent of the increase and giving 25 percent back to the lender. This practice is called the subjective markup (Mayer, 2003). The problem with this is the potential for racial discrimination is great. African Americans can be charged more for the initial interest rate and are more likely to have the subjective interest rate imposed and increased.

Some plaintiffs, who were the African Americans, hired an expert, Mark Cohen, to conduct research on both GMAC and NMAC and their lending practices. Following an analysis of the data, Cohen (2003) found that:

1. When a markup is imposed, 53.4 percent of African Americans receive a markup compared to 28.2 percent of Whites.
2. When the size of the markup is examined for both groups, African Americans' markup is 2.7 times the amount for Whites—$656 to $244.
3. African American borrowers who receive a subjective markup are charged on average $1,229 compared to only $867 for Whites.
4. Among 1.5 million GMAC borrowers, a total of $421.6 million was paid in subjective markup. African Americans paid $83.9 million or 19.9 percent of the total although African Americans make up only 8.5 percent of the customer base.
5. In Tennessee, where the lawsuit was filed, African Americans on average paid $929 compared to $317 for Whites, the highest difference.

6. Over 12,000 GMAC customers paid more than $3,000 in subjective markup. African Americans make up 33.5 percent of borrowers who paid more than $3,000 although they represent only 8.5 percent of the borrower pool.

Cohen (2003) reported that he conducted numerous analyses of the data and concluded that the disparate impact against African Americans could not be explained by creditworthiness or other legitimate business factors. Perhaps based on these analyses, GMAC agreed to settle the lawsuit. Although details of the settlement were not widely reported, reports are that GMAC would give African Americans more information about how interest rates are set and limit the flexibility given to dealers in deciding markups. Early in the case, a court of appeals ruled that the case could not be tried as a class action because individual loans were too different, and as a result, money damages were deleted from the case (Mayer, 2004).

Conclusion

Of course, many Whites and some conservative African Americans will reject the notion that events after slavery and for most of the twentieth century have anything to do with African Americans' current economic status. Yet, one must acknowledge that the taking of land from a people emerging from slavery with nothing and destroying nascent African American businesses had a devastating effect on African Americans' economic well-being. African Americans' economic growth was seriously stifled by racism.

For example, many current White businesses have their beginnings in the late 1800s or early 1900s, such as K-Mart and Sears. Often, these businesses began with some merchant pushing a cart selling items from it. If these businesses were owned by foreign Whites, such as Italians, Irish, or Jews, they might have encountered harassment, but they were not attacked like African Americans were attacked. Possibly, the Peoples' Grocery Store that was owned by three African Americans in the late 1800s in Memphis, Tennessee, could have grown to a major supermarket chain, like Kroger or Safeway. These African American owners could have left their heirs a thriving business and perhaps created a foundation for aiding other African Americans educationally and economically.

Similarly, farming land could have been developed and food grown and sold commercially. Some African Americans could have become chicken, pork, and cattle barons and left their heirs thriving businesses. Tyson Foods, for example, had sales of $24.5 billion in 2003 and is the largest producer of chicken, pork, and beef in the world. It started, however, in 1931 when John Tyson hauled hay, fruit, and chicken for local growers. In 1935, he transported a battered truckload of chickens from Arkansas to Chicago and began his chicken empire. With little or no formal education or experience, African Americans were doing well in businesses shortly after leaving slavery. They took care of the land and the farm animals and for sure some of them had the same or more entrepreneurial spirit as John Tyson.

Some African Americans had lots which were stolen and those lots that were located in the downtown areas could have led to commercial parking lots, such as Allbright Parking that is located nationwide in cities and airports.

Racial covenants that required that White owners do not sell or rent property to African Americans, mortgage discrimination, and insurance discrimination impeded African Americans' homeownership. According to Ross and Yinger (2002), "homeownership is the most commonly used method for wealth accumulation, and it is widely viewed as critical for access to the nicest communities and the best local public services, especially education" (p. 1). African Americans, more than any other racial group, were denied this opportunity for a long, long time.

Presently, some African Americans are doing better economically. Some African Americans have found very recent financial successes in the business field, but discrimination still exists in opportunities. A few years back, two of the best defensive linemen in professional football played on the same team. One was White and one was African American. The White player admitted that after retirement, he was given more financial opportunities than his African American counterpart.

American Americans have found more recent successes in the entertainment fields—music, sports, and television. These are really very recent advances, occurring within the last ten years or so. Some of these entertainers have contributed millions to the education of African Americans, such as Oprah Winfrey and Bill Cosby. Critics of African Americans' lack of wealth should not expect instantaneous success as if African Americans had the same opportunities as Whites and other ethnic groups. Racism, not the lack of resourcefulness or reliance upon the federal government, is the cause of African Americans playing economic catch-up.

7

African Americans and Reparations

CREDIT FOR THE REPARATION movement for African Americans has been attributed to Dr. Imari Obadele, founder of the Republic of New Africa. In the early 1970s, he demanded that the United States pay reparations of $400 billion for the ravages of slavery (Phipps, 2001). In 1988, the movement for reparation became more formalized. Then, Dr. Obadele and other reparationists established the National Coalition of Blacks for Reparations in America and began to champion this issue and support litigation in the courts (Phipps, 2001).

However, Judge F. Michael Higginbotham (2003) has stated that newly freed African Americans and a few supporters pressed Congress for reparations in 1860. Bills were passed in Congress, but all were vetoed by President Andrew Johnson (Higginbotham, 2003). On the legal front, Charles Ogletree (2003) also described a long history of efforts to seek reparations and noted that a lawsuit was filed and subsequently dismissed in the court in 1915. Demands for reparations came from former slaves, abolitionists, and some members of the old Republican party, which at that time was the comparable to the current Democratic party.

In 1866, Senator Thaddeus Stevens gave a speech on the floor of the Senate calling for forty acres and a mule for African Americans (Higginbotham, 2003). The legislation did not pass but unfulfilled promises were made to African Americans that they would get forty acres and a mule, which later became a joke among African Americans about the many broken promises of Whites. Spike Lee, the African American movie producer, named his company "40 Acres and a Mule."

The movement for reparations was initially embraced by only a few African Americans and hardly any Whites (Daniels, 1990). The movement began to become more intense when African Americans took note that Congress passed the Civil Liberties Act of 1988, which provided for payment of reparations for the internment of thousands of Japanese Americans during World War II (Bryan, 2003). Further, Jewish Americans had successfully pressed for reparations from some European businesses.

Perhaps feeling overlooked and marginalized, Representative John Conyers, an African American representative from Michigan, introduced legislation to study the impact of slavery on African Americans and to institute payment of reparations to African Americans in the event that the study found that slavery has a current effect on them. This bill failed to get out of committee, but Conyers has introduced it every year since 1988 (*In re African-American Slave Descendants Litigation*, 2004).

However, there has been a steadily growing number of voices who have sought to disclose and study issues surrounding slavery. For example, California passed a law that required insurance companies doing business in the state to disclose slaves that it had insured and slaveowners who purchased policies from them (Aubry, 2002). Also, the president of Brown University has ordered a study of the extent to which Brown University benefited from slavery. Most recently, the University of Alabama has acknowledged that slaves built portions of the university, and it intends to place a marker on the graves of slaves buried near the University of Alabama ("University of Alabama Moves to Acknowledge Slavery Links," 2004), which is ironically the same school in which George Wallace stood in the door to block two African Americans from entering. This chapter discusses reparations, contemporary precedents for African Americans receiving reparations, arguments against and for reparations, a rebuttal to criticisms against reparations, and the legal case involving the lawsuits filed by African Americans.

Definition of Reparations and the Restitution Principle

Reparations are compensatory and punitive payments made from one state to another state (Zweig, 2001). America (2002) explained the restitution principle as the principle that whenever a social group, nation, or race determines that its past behavior was wrong and immoral and these wrong and immoral behaviors produced unjust benefits, then it is wrong to retain those benefits. It is incumbent to make restitution by some form of explicit redistributive public or private action. Slavery was a significant factor in manufacturing, mining, agriculture, and services and thus produced unjust benefits for Whites (America, 2002).

Slavery also produced unjust benefits for some insurance companies. For example, a particular slave once ran away and refused to surrender when caught. The bounty hunters killed him. The owner of the slave subsequently attempted to collect an insurance policy from North Carolina Mutual Life Insurance Company. The policy, however, stated that no benefits would be paid if the slave died by means of invasion, insurrection, riot, civil commotion, military action, or by the criminal justice system. Because the slave was killed in an attempt to return him, the owner wanted to collect the $500 benefit. The policyholder lost in the lower court, but the Supreme Court of North Carolina ruled in his favor and ordered the insurance to pay the amount plus interest (*Spruill v. The North Carolina Mutual Life Insurance Company*, 1853).

Reflective of the restitution principle, Robinson (2001) stated that slave labor built the White House, Congress, and the Lincoln Monument, yet there is no attribution anywhere to the slaves. For instance, the U.S. government requested one hundred slaves from nearby slaveowners. These owners were paid five dollars per slave per month. These slaves cleared land between the then–White House and the Capitol. They also helped to construct an important symbol of freedom—the Statue of Freedom that sits on the top of the Capitol. The statue was designed in Rome, Italy, in 1856 by Thomas Crawford, who was paid $3,000. In 1863, the statue was cast in bronze by a Maryland foundry owned by Clark Mills. The U.S. government paid Mills $23,736. However, the actual work was done by one of Clark Mills' slaves, Philip Reed. Philip Reed and other slaves transported the Statue of Freedom, which was in five pieces, with each piece weighing over a ton. On the Capitol grounds, it was assembled to ensure the pieces fit—a task that took thirty-one days. Then, it was disassembled and hoisted up to the top of the Capitol (Robinson, 2001).

The irony is that the Statue of Freedom was bronzed by a slave. Throughout Washington, DC, there are symbols touting liberty, democracy, and freedom that Africans helped to construct, but there is no recognition in, or upon, these buildings. Robinson does not suggest that African Americans should acquire ownership of the Statue of Freedom, the White House, Congress, and the Lincoln Monument. Instead, there should be a public acknowledgment that slave labor helped create many of these historical figures, instead of simply ignoring the contribution of slaves.

Contemporary Precedents for African Americans Receiving Reparations

The precedent for the successful paying of reparations in contemporary society is what Germany had to pay to the Jews and the State of Israel. After the

Allies defeated Germany and occupied Germany, they directed that the new German government make restitutions to the Jews. However, no legal precedents existed for reparations because generally reparations are payments made between states. Another legal difficulty was that Jews were made heirless by the atrocities of the Holocaust, and property in which there are no heirs reverts to the state. The Jews had no state to press reparation payments, but talks were underway with several Jewish organizations on paying to and rehabilitating the lives of Jewish people.

Taking the lead role, the Conference on Jewish Material Claims Against Germany pressed for financial restitutions by the new Federal Republic of Germany, but these early talks did not produce any tangible results. After the State of Israel was created, it became the official state with which to negotiate with Germany for the payment of reparations. On September 10, 1952, an agreement was reached among the Federal Republic of Germany, the State of Israel, and the Conference on Jewish Material Claims Against Germany. According to Zweig (2001), "reparations, restitution and indemnification together transferred vast amounts of money to individual Jews, to the State of Israel and to Jewish communities throughout the world" (p. 11). Since World War II, 115 billion DM (Deutsche Marks) or about 55.2 billion dollars have been paid to Jews through reparations, restitutions, and indemnification, with the most being paid as indemnification. Rehabilitation projects for Jews have been funded throughout the world, including the United States, Great Britain, Latin America, Australia, and other countries. Funds have been expended for community and youth centers, youth shelters, vacation colonies, medical facilities, religious institutions, cemeteries, canteens, sheltered workshops, and sundry others (Zweig, 2001).

Later, numerous Jews sued several Swiss banks for the return of Jewish funds kept following the Holocaust and the destruction of records of accounts held by Jews. The Claims Resolution Tribunal was established to study the issue of missing records and determine how many accounts had belonged to Jews. Although the case was complicated by the lack of direct proof, circumstantial evidence suggested that missing bank records probably were those of Jews killed in the Holocaust. A settlement was reached in 2000 and approved by the U.S. district court and the Second Circuit Court of Appeals. In accordance with the settlement, $150,589,699 was paid to 1,934 claimants in the Deposited Assets Class in connection with 1,802 bank accounts found by the Claims Resolution Tribunal to have belonged to victims of the Holocaust; $214,483,050 was paid to 148,609 surviving members of the Slave Labor Class I; $45,000 to 45 members of the Slave Labor Class II; $7,804,050 to 2,898 surviving members of the Refugee Class; and $205,000,000 to needy survivors of the Holocaust through application of the cy pres doctrine to the Looted Assets Class (*In re: Holocaust Victim Assets Litigation*, 2004).

In another lawsuit, several Jewish persons sued several banks and financial institutions in France. The plaintiffs contended that they should be compensated for the defendants' alleged wrongful taking and failure to return money to Jews in France during World War II and after the war. The banks filed a motion to dismiss the lawsuit, which was denied by a U.S. district court in New York. Then, the defendant banks sought a protective order to limit discovery, arguing that the production of the many records would be oppressive and burdensome. Also, the defendants argued that discovery should proceed according to the Hague Convention and not the Federal Rules of Civil Procedure. The Hague Convention refers to the name for the Convention for taking evidence abroad in civil or commercial cases. However, the U.S. Supreme Court had ruled in a case in 1987, *Societe Nationale Industrielle Aerospatiale v. United States*, that the Hague Convention did not supplant the Federal Rules of Civil Procedure, permitting U.S. citizens to sue a French aircraft manufacturer whose plane crashed. Accordingly, the U.S. district court permitted discovery according to federal rules (*Bodner et al. v. Banque Paribas*, 2000).

Another precedent for African Americans receiving reparations is the Civil Liberties Act of 1988 (Bryan, 2003), which was for the benefit of Japanese Americans who were put in internment camps. Signed into law by President Ronald Reagan, the Act was:

(1) to acknowledge the fundamental injustice of the evacuation, relocation, and internment of United States citizens and permanent resident aliens of Japanese ancestry during World War II;

(2) to apologize on behalf of the people of the United States for the evacuation, relocation, and internment of such citizens and permanent resident aliens;

(3) to provide for a public education fund to finance efforts to inform the public about the internment of such individuals so as to prevent the recurrence of any similar event;

(4) to make restitution to those individuals of Japanese ancestry who were interned;

(5) to make restitution to Aleut residents of the Pribilof Islands and the Aleutian Islands west of Unimak Island, in settlement of United States obligations in equity and at law, for:

(A) injustices suffered and unreasonable hardships endured while those Aleut residents were under United States control during World War II;

(B) personal property taken or destroyed by United States forces during World War II;

(C) community property, including community church property, taken or destroyed by United States forces during World War II; and

  (D) traditional village lands on Attu Island not rehabilitated after
       World War II for Aleut occupation or other productive use;
  (6) to discourage the occurrence of similar injustices and violations of civil
       liberties in the future; and
  (7) to make more credible and sincere any declaration of concern by the
       United States over violations of human rights committed by other na-
       tions (Civil Liberties Act of 1988).

To achieve the objectives of the Civil Liberties Act of 1988, Congress allocated
the sum of $1,650,000,000 (Civil Liberties Act of 1988).

Bryan (2003) further argued that a precedent exists as a result of the Rosewood Massacre that occurred in Sumner, Florida, in 1923. A White woman
claimed that an African American male had assaulted and robbed her. The
prime suspect was thought to be an escaped prisoner. The sheriff and a group
of White men searched for him. The men came to Rosewood, a thriving
African American community. Six African Americans and two White men
were killed in an altercation, and this scrimmage led to a full-scale assault on
Rosewood. When the attack had ended, the entire Rosewood community,
consisting of businesses, homes, and churches, was destroyed, and all the
African Americans were either killed or forced to leave the area. In 1994, the
Florida legislature passed a law to compensate the survivors of the Rosewood
Massacre, which it admitted was caused in part by the local government. A
somewhat paltry sum of $150,000 was allocated for survivors. In addition,
scholarship and research funds were created for future African Americans
(Bryan, 2003).

Arguments against and for Reparations for African Americans

As expected, strong opposition has come from many Whites and some
African Americans about reparations for African Americans. One of the initial conditions for reparations is for a government to officially apologize for
harm caused to a group. Although pressed for an official apology, President
Clinton, a moderate Democrat who enjoyed strong support from African
American voters, refused to issue a formal apology. At that time, a larger percentage of White voters was opposed to the American government apologizing for slavery. As some conservative Whites have stated, the wrongs of the
past cannot be righted by reparations, but apparently this view only applies
to African Americans. It was not the view expressed for Jews or Japanese
Americans.

Philosophical Arguments against Reparations

Perhaps the strongest vocal critic of reparations is David Horowitz, a reputed former liberal from the 1960s whom some African Americans now call a racist, who has attacked the idea of reparations for African Americans. Horowitz (2002) not only wrote a book critical of reparations, but he also took out advertisements in college campus newspapers stating reparations are a bad idea for African Americans. Horowitz does not feel that reparations for Jews for the Holocaust and for Japanese Americans are precedents for African Americans receiving reparations. In his advertisement, Horowitz (2003) pointed out ten reasons why reparations are wrong or bad for African Americans. Although Horowitz has taken offense to how he has been criticized and attacked, his views indeed are misleading, wrong, and false. Horowitz wrote that "during the slavery era, many blacks were free men or slave-owners themselves, yet the reparation claimants make no distinction between the roles blacks actually played in the injustice itself" (Horowitz, 2001).

Another offensive statement made by Horowitz is that America has already paid reparations to African Americans through the Great Society programs in the 1960s and welfare payments, which have amounted to trillions of dollars. In addition, he charged that African Americans have benefited from racial preferences in the form of contracts, job placements, and educational admissions. He asserted that "if trillion dollar restitutions and a wholesale rewriting of American law (in order to accommodate racial preferences) for African Americans is not enough to achieve a 'healing,' what will?" (Horowitz, 2002)

As expected, Horowitz's position and views, which were published in several campus newspapers, invoked a barrage of criticisms, which he attempted to refute. Horowitz (2003) wrote:

> The reparations claim is too tendentious to be taken seriously. Both the injured parties and the perpetrators are dead. With respect to private companies, the tort is too old. As respects to the government, the tort is too old and the government that is being sued is not the injuring party—the Confederacy—but a government that freed the slaves at great human and material cost and that has provided trillions of dollars to African Americans who are disadvantaged. The reparations tort is frivolous and if brought by lawyers on behalf of any group but African Americans would be laughed out of court, while counsel would be sanctioned under Rule 11.

As stated in the Federal Rules of Civil Procedures, Rule 11 provides sanctions for a plaintiff who has filed a meritless, frivolous, or harassing lawsuit.

Philosophical Arguments in Support of Reparations

While there is indeed an historical account of an African American family owning slaves in Louisiana, this is an anomaly and certainly was not the norm. Numerous laws, such as the Black Codes, severely restricted African Americans' lives during and after slavery. Banks would not lend money to African Americans to buy slaves, as banks did for White plantation owners. Also, numerous laws prevented African Americans from buying or acquiring property, which slaves were then, and those laws restricting ownership persisted and grew after slavery up until the 1940s. As Boyle (2003) pointed out, some African Americans who were freed were able to save and buy their relatives' freedom, which is not the same as African Americans simply buying slaves. Horowitz's argument in this sense would be the same as saying that Oskar Schindler, who bought his Jewish workers from the Germans to save them from the gas chambers, was a slaveowner.

Explaining theoretically why White America is opposed to reparations, Harris (2003) wrote that support for reparations violates several norms that purport to exist in America—self-reliance, private property, and equal opportunity. Furthermore, some individuals might believe in reparations, but are afraid to support it because it violates the norms of society. Before John Conyers introduced his bill to study the effects of slavery, Representative Tony Hall proposed a bill in 1997 for the American government to apologize for slavery, but this bill was summarily rejected and caused Representative Hall to receive considerable hate mail and nasty telephone calls to his office. Hall's bill came at a time when the American government had apologized to the Japanese Americans interned during World War II. One critic stated that the United States had gone apology crazy by apologizing to indigenous Hawaiians, Guatemalans, African Americans used as guinea pigs in the Tuskegee experiment, and Rosewood (Harris, 2003).

Further Observations and Arguments Overlooked Regarding Reparations

Horowitz has made some outlandish statements regarding African Americans and what African Americans owe to America. Among the statements were that White soldiers during the Civil War gave up their lives to free the slaves and President Lincoln gave his life by signing the Emancipation Proclamation. The Civil War was not fought principally to free the slaves. It was to preserve the Union. President Lincoln wrote a letter to a New York newspaper in which he stated that his intent was not to save or destroy slavery and that if he could save the Union by preserving slavery, he would (Williams, 1998). In a speech in 1858, President Lincoln said:

> I will say here, while upon this subject, that I have no purpose directly or indirectly to interfere with the institution of slavery in the States where it exists. I believe I have no lawful right to do so, and I have no inclination to do so. I have no purpose to introduce political and social equality between the white and the black races. There is a physical difference between the two, which in my judgment will probably forever forbid their living together upon the footing of perfect equality, and inasmuch as it becomes necessity that there must be a difference, I, as well as Judge Douglas, am in favor of the race to which I belong, having the superior position. (Basler, 1953, p. 16)

Turning to the statement that many White Union soldiers died to free the slaves, this claim too is dubious. President Lincoln's aim was to preserve the Union and White males signed up to help preserve the Union. Many Northern White men saw Southerners as traitors who were out to destroy this country by trying to break away. Their aim was to prevent this perceived destruction from occurring. Supporting this view, many Union soldiers highly resented African American soldiers fighting for the Union and many of them stated that they would not fight alongside African Americans.

According to Alt and Alt (2002),

> Many Union soldiers were among the opponents of Negro participation [in the Civil War]. They and the civilian population predicted that enlisting blacks as soldiers would lead to racial equality with whites. This would be an intolerable situation, with whites refusing to volunteer for service or deserting if they were already in the army. One young white officer assigned to report to a black unit was told by a staff officer that "they did not want any nigger soldiers in the Army of the Potomac," and a general said to him, "I am sorry . . . that you are going to serve with Negroes. I think it is a disgrace to the army to make soldiers of them." (Alt & Alt, 2002, pp. 36–37)

Considerable double standards exist in discussions of reparations. For example, Horowitz (2003) claimed that Jesse Jackson and other African Americans used political pressure to shake down Texaco and receive a settlement of $176.1 million for African American workers, and insinuated that this was some type of political extortion by African Americans. Yet, according to Bazyler (2002), political pressure on behalf of Jewish litigants was paramount to force European banks and insurance companies to settle with Jewish plaintiffs suing foreign corporations. New York Senator Alfonse D'Amato conducted hearings on European banks, and threats to boycott Swiss banks by various local and state governments were made if the Swiss banks did not settle with the Jewish plaintiffs. Initially, the Swiss banks indicated that they were going to vigorously contest the lawsuits, but as the pressure rose, they became more amenable to settlement. Asked why the banks changed their positions, Rabbi Marvin Heir, Director of the Simon Wiesenthal Center in Los Angeles, said, "they were pressured into it. Without the pressure, without Senator D'Amato's banking committee, without the threat of sanctions, the Holocaust survivors would have gotten nothing" (Bazyler, 2002, p. 17).

Horowitz (2003), further, wrote that lawsuits over reparations for African Americans are ridiculous because slave victims and slave owners are long dead and African Americans cannot sue for dead African American victims. Yet, this argument is legally incorrect. Relatives and estates have long sued for dead people in this country. Parents sue for the death of their dead or injured adult children and estates sue on behalf of the dead. One of the plaintiffs in the civil lawsuit against O. J. Simpson was Nicole Simpson's estate and a judgment was awarded to her estate.

More importantly, African Americans following slavery who had been enslaved had no legal standing to sue. Following the end of slavery in 1863, African Americans could not sue. They certainly could not sue for reparations prior to 1863 because the U.S. Supreme Court had ruled in 1857 that Dred Scott had no standing to sue over his freedom. After 1863, the courts were very hostile to African Americans for many, many decades. Thus, it is disingenuous for critics to charge that African Americans waited too long to file lawsuits for reparations.

Horowitz (2003) claimed that his argument that African Americans have received reparations from the American government through welfare and social programs during the 1960s, amounting to trillions of dollars, has been conceded or tacitly endorsed by some of his critics. But these African American critics of him want more dollars in the form of reparations. However, this author concedes nothing and wholly rejects such a conclusion that welfare has benefited African Americans. Horowitz unabashedly states that African Americans have received trillions of dollars, and such an assertion is wrong and racist. Many people believe incorrectly that only African Americans receive welfare. Although a disproportionate number of African Americans receive welfare or public assistance, the actual number of White people receiving welfare is greater. Latinos also have received welfare and poor Whites have long received welfare. African Americans have as much right to public assistance as any other group, and public assistance for African Americans cannot be reparations for them, but not others.

Table 7.1, compiled by the U.S. Department of Health and Human Services (Lower-Basch, 2000), shows the race of families receiving AFDC (Aid to Families with Dependent Children) and TANF (Temporary Assistance for Needy

Families) from 1985 to 1999. As shown by the data, Whites make up a sizeable percentage of individuals receiving welfare. In 1992, 1993, and 1994, Whites were the largest percentage of individuals receiving welfare. If Whites, Latinos, Asians, and Native Americans were combined, this group, compared to African Americans, received the largest amount of welfare. Hence, if welfare is reparations, then others received the lion's share of the reparations. Furthermore, if welfare is reparations as Horowitz contends, then why are Whites receiving reparations?

Horowitz also has made a horrendous charge that African Americans are racists just for asking for reparations. In his newspaper advertisement, he gave "Ten Reasons Why Reparations for Blacks Is a Bad Idea for Blacks—and Racist Too" (Horowitz, 2001). He did not call Jews or Japanese Americans racists for asking for reparations and claimed that Jews and Japanese Americans had just claims for reparations because they were identifiable victims. However, this is not entirely true. He also said that it would be unjust to force innocent Whites who have never owned slaves to pay reparations. However, the $1,650,000,000 that Congress allocated for Japanese Americans did not come just from Whites. African Americans pay taxes too, and some of their tax monies were part of this $1,650,000,000. African Americans did not put the Japanese in internment camps, yet they paid a portion of the reparations.

TABLE 7.1
Percentages of AFDC/TANF Families by Race from 1985 to 1999

Fiscal Year	White	African American	Latino	Asian	Native American	Unknown
			Race of Parent			
1985	40.8	41.6	13.6	2.4	1.2	2.2
1986	39.7	40.7	14.4	2.3	1.3	1.4
1987	38.8	39.8	15.5	2.6	1.3	2.0
1988	38.8	39.8	15.7	2.4	1.4	1.9
1989	38.4	40.1	15.9	2.7	1.3	1.5
1990	38.1	39.7	16.6	2.8	1.3	1.5
1991	38.1	38.8	17.4	2.8	1.3	1.6
1992	38.9	37.2	17.8	2.8	1.4	2.0
1993	38.3	36.6	18.5	2.9	1.3	2.2
1994	37.4	36.4	19.9	2.9	1.3	2.1
1995	35.6	37.2	20.7	3.0	1.3	2.2
1996	35.9	37.2	20.7	3.0	1.3	2.2
1997	34.5	37.3	22.5	3.3	1.3	1.1
1998	32.7	39.0	22.2	3.4	1.5	1.3
1999	30.5	38.3	24.5	3.6	1.5	1.6

Moreover, the reparations paid to the Jews were unprecedented, legally and politically. Many Jews who were not citizens of Germany benefited from the reparations that Germany paid, and these Jews were not victims of the Holocaust, according to Michael J. Bazyler (2002). Horowitz charged that only direct Jewish victims or their immediate families received reparations, but this is not true. Individual Jews received reparations from Germany, but also the State of Israel and Jewish communities throughout the world. If some Jews after the Holocaust immigrated to Israel and they were direct victims, then the money should have gone directly to them, not the State of Israel. Some of these funds came to the United States, where there was no Holocaust. While it may not be widely known, it could be that some of the Jewish resources (i.e., community and youth shelters, vacation colonies, medical facilities, religious institutions, cemeteries, and canteens) in the United States were funded in part or in whole by restitutions from Germany and benefited Jews in the United States who were not victims of the Holocaust.

The same is true with job training programs with the Great Society. Funds for job training did not go to African Americans exclusively. When money was being allocated for the Great Society, White politicians and White mayors controlled these funds and Whites received large portions of these moneys. Numerous Whites received administrative jobs during the Great Society. If there indeed were trillions of dollars being spent on welfare and social programs, the chief beneficiaries were Whites, not African Americans.

We see similar evidence with affirmative action for minority businesses—another way in which Horowitz incorrectly says African Americans have received reparations. Yet, reports have indicated that many times, Whites benefit from minority businesses by creating businesses with African Americans as fronts.

Last, African Americans have not benefited greatly from affirmative action. Affirmative action simply encourages hiring authorities to do more in terms of recruiting ethnic minorities and women before reducing the pool of candidates. Affirmative action does not guarantee jobs to African Americans. Horowitz is incorrect in declaring that African Americans have had laws tailored to benefit them. In the manner in which Horowitz implies, the main beneficiaries of affirmative action are White females. Presently, females make up the largest percentage (i.e., 50 percent) of law school admissions (Gasner, 2004) and at some schools the percentage is more than 50 percent (Schroering, 2003; Suffolk University Law School, 2004). Women make up 50 percent of admissions to medical schools (Schevitz, 2003). Certainly, these are primarily White females. An Athletic Director has stated that the chief beneficiaries of Title IX, which is a form of affirmative action for women athletes, have been White females.

Whatever small benefits that affirmative action has produced for African Americans educationally are not due to some notion of reparations but simply because it is just and due. Moreover, African Americans paid taxes for years, and some of their tax dollars went to White, segregated universities and colleges. Students at public institutions do not pay the full cost for getting a college education. In fact, the largest percentage of the cost to educate students comes from state and federal budgets. For years, African Americans paid taxes to support higher education, but their children could not go to those schools. Also, African American veterans from World War II were entitled to a college education because of their service under the G.I. Bill, but none of them could go to these universities and colleges.

Attempts at Legal Redress for Descendants of African American Slaves in the Courts

Several African American plaintiffs filed nine lawsuits, which were consolidated and moved to the U.S. District Court for the Northern District of Illinois, against several major corporations, including Brown & Williamson Tobacco Company, R. J. Reynolds Tobacco Company, CSX Railroads, Fleet Boston Financial Corporation, Norfolk Southern Railway Company, Canadian National Railroad Company, the Society of Lloyds or Lloyd's of London, and Aetna Insurance Company. The basis of these lawsuits was to hold these companies financially responsible for benefiting and profiting from the institution of slavery in the United States (*In re African-American Slave Descendants Litigation*, 2004).

U.S. District Court Judge Charles R. Norgle heard the case, and in his decision, he briefly summarized the history of slavery in Africa and its expansion in the New World before discussing the legal issues that the case presented. By his accounts, slavery had taken a stronger hold in Brazil, Mexico, Peru, Cuba, Haiti, Jamaica, the British West Indies, and Dutch Guyana than it had in Colonial America. But slavery grew in Colonial America, surpassing slavery in other countries and making the United States the leader of slave labor in the New World. Slavery became the dominant economic force in the United States. Two reasons existed for this economic growth of slavery. One, slavery was very inexpensive in that slaveowners did not have to pay wages to workers. Two, slaveowners were permitted to use unrestrained force and violence to transform ancient modes of labor into a new industrial discipline (*In re African-American Slave Descendants Litigation*, 2004).

One way in which to interpret the latter reason is that the plantation system was allowed to work slaves in a manner that an owner could not do with regular employees. A free white male, for example, could hire himself to who-ever was willing to pay him the most and leave when he wanted to leave. If he was sick, he might not work that day. Slaves, however, did not have this choice. Slaveowners could literally work slaves to death, increasing the wealth of the slaveowner. Then, there was another major economic benefit for owners of slaves; they included the offspring of slaves. Children born into slavery be-came economic assets too, either to be forced to work or to be sold.

Support for slavery existed among vast numbers of citizens and within the law for a long period of time. Article I, Section 9 of the U.S. Constitution was long interpreted as a restraint upon Congress to not interfere with the insti-tution of slavery. Congress could limit the importation of slaves after 1808, but it could not interfere with the internal slave trade within the Southern states. Additional congressional support for slavery existed when Congress passed the Fugitive Slave Act in 1850. This act gave slaveowners and their rep-resentatives the right to pursue runaway slaves in another state and to retrieve these slaves. The Fugitive Slave Act provided fines and imprisonment for any-one who helped a runaway slave and stated that both law enforcement and or-dinary citizens were legally bound to help or aid in the capture of runaway slaves (*In re African-American Slave Descendants Litigation*, 2004).

The plaintiffs' lawsuits alleged nine counts, which were:

Count 1	The complaint alleged conspiracy by the defendants to en-gage in conduct within their respective industries conducive to perpetuation of slavery.
Count 2	The complaint demanded an accounting of defendants' cor-porate records so that a just and fair accounting could be made about the profits from the slave trade.
Count 3	The complaint alleged crimes against humanity.
Count 4	The complaint alleged piracy and the relief sought consisted of an accounting of profits earned from slave labor, a con-structive trust imposed on such profits, restitution, equitable disgorgement, and punitive damages.
Count 5	The complaint alleged intentional infliction of emotional dis-tress by rape, breeding, torture, abuse, and the spread of racist beliefs.
Count 6	The complaint alleged conversion of slave labor into slave-owners' property.
Count 7	The complaint alleged unjust enrichment from the labor of slaves.
Count 8	The complaint alleged as a result of the defendants' conduct, Title 42 U.S.C. § 1982 was violated. (This statute says that "all

citizens of the United States shall have the same right, in every State or Territory, as is enjoyed by White citizens thereof to inherit, purchase, lease, sell, hold, and convey real and personal property.")

Count 9   The complaint alleged that because slaves were not citizens, the Alien Tort Claims Act provided a source for relief based on the violation of international law.

Counts 10–14   The complaint alleged various violations of state laws.

The defendants filed a joint motion for dismissal of the lawsuit. They argued on four grounds or reasons for why the plaintiffs' lawsuit should be dismissed: (1) The plaintiffs had no standing to file the lawsuit; (2) the plaintiffs' claims presented a nonjusticiable political question; (3) the plaintiffs failed to state any cognizable claim; and (4) the plaintiffs' claims were time-barred.

The U.S. district court found all the defendants' arguments to be legally sound and valid. In conclusion, the judge wrote:

It is beyond debate that slavery has caused tremendous suffering and inelimimable scars throughout our Nation's history. However, plaintiffs' claims, as alleged in their complaint, fail based on numerous well-settled legal principles. First, Plaintiffs' claims are beyond the constitutional authority of this court. Without alleging any specific connection between themselves and the named defendants, plaintiffs lack essential constitutional standing requirements to bring their claims. Second, prudential limitations prohibit the court from deciding such broad questions of social importance when such claims are brought on behalf of absent third parties, as Plaintiffs attempt here. Third, the long-standing and well-reasoned political question doctrine bars the court from deciding the issue of slavery reparations, an issue that has been historically and constitutionally committed to the Legislative and Executive branches of our government. Fourth, Plaintiffs claims are untimely. Conceding that many of the torts alleged in the Complaint occurred prior to the formal end of slavery, Plaintiffs fail to show how any of these claims fall within the applicable statutes of limitation. Finally, under the rules of procedure which guide the federal judicial system, Plaintiffs Complaint fails to state a claim upon which relief can be granted, a serious defect the court cannot overlook regardless how egregious the circumstances giving rise to the claims.

In summary, Plaintiffs' attempt to bring these claims more than a century after the end of the Civil War and the formal abolition of slavery fails; this determination is consistent with the position taken by numerous courts which have considered the issue over the last century. Ultimately, the legal obstacles prohibiting judicial resolution of such claims cannot be circumvented by the courts. Moreover, from the onset of the Civil War until present, the historical record clearly shows that the President and Congress have the constitutional authority to determine the nature and scope of the relief sought in this case, not the courts. This is manifested in the signing of the Emancipation Proclamation; the enactment of the Thirteenth, Fourteenth, and Fifteenth Amendments to the United States Constitution; and the promulgation of over a century of civil rights legislation. (*In re African-American Slave Descendants Litigation,* 2004)

Conclusion

African Americans begrudge neither Jews' nor Japanese Americans' receiving reparations. Attempting to convince African Americans that their case is vastly different from the cases involving Jews and Japanese Americans is demeaning and insulting. Furthermore, calling African Americans racists for advocating for reparations is preposterous. A number of reasons, however, exist for the reluctance of the American government to consider seriously reparations for African Americans. Many of them have already been stated, including the large dollar figure due to African Americans that some advocates have stated exceeds over a trillion dollars. Also, the government might believe that other groups will step forward, such as Native Americans who can document genocidal practices by the American government (Bradford, 2003). Hence, reparations for African Americans may not materialize but the demands are morally right.

8

African Americans, Employment Discrimination, and Legal Justice

---

EARLY ON, THE COURTS WERE NOT friendly toward African American plaintiffs, and many of the earlier decisions, such as the Dred Scott case and *Plessy v. Ferguson*, were adverse to African Americans. Then also the courts were frequently inconsistent in their decisions, ruling one way for some individuals and then another way for African Americans. In the 1960s some decisions seemingly were legal victories for African Americans. However, as a whole, the courts have made justice for African Americans more difficult to achieve. This chapter discusses the law in employment decisions and shows differences in rulings when the plaintiffs are African Americans. Employment is a vital area for all individuals and competition for this resource has led to violence and laws against job discrimination. Also, the U.S. Supreme Court recognizes a job as property under the Fourteenth Amendment to the U.S. Constitution (*Board of Regents v. Roth*, 1972).

Legal Standards for Employment Discrimination

In 1973, the U.S. Supreme Court established the test to be used by lower courts in deciding whether an African American can establish racial discrimination in employment (*McDonnell Douglas Corp. v. Green*, 1973). This case has far-reaching implications, applying to initial employment and promotions. In this case, Percy H. Green, an African American, contended that his employer, McDonnell Douglas, engaged in discrimination in employment. Green, a mechanic, was laid off, which Green thought was tainted by racism. He protested and allegedly organized a "stall-in," in which several cars blocked the entrance to the plant during the morning shift change. Green was subsequently arrested. Later, when McDonnell Douglas began rehiring laid-off workers, Green applied but was rejected. Thereupon, Green sued, alleging racial discrimination. McDonnell Douglas' defense was that it did not rehire Green because of his illegal activity against the plant.

The U.S. Supreme Court unanimously decided how the courts were to decide racial discrimination cases filed under Title VII of the Civil Rights Act. It ruled that the complainant must carry the initial burden in establishing a prima facie case of racial discrimination. Such an establishment can be made by showing that he or she (a) belongs to a racial minority; (b) that he or she applied for a job for which the employer was seeking applications; (c) that he or she was rejected despite being qualified for the position; and (d) that after the complainant's rejection, the employer continued to seek applications. Once the complainant establishes these facts, the burden shifts to the employer to show some legitimate, nondiscriminatory reason for the employer's adverse decision to the complainant. Then, the complainant must be given an opportunity to show that the employer's purported decision is a pretext for a racially discriminatory decision (*McDonnell Douglas Corp. v. Green*, 1973). Thus, African Americans must establish all these criteria to prevail.

Illustrations of the Use of the *McDonnell Douglas* Standard

Numerous courts in deciding racial discrimination cases have used this decision to rule against African Americans. Simply, it is quite easy to proffer some reason for not hiring or promoting an African American. In Green's case, Green's illegal activity was cited. But it could easily be having a year or two more experience, having one type of degree or another, being a better public speaker, or having better administrative skills.

By illustration, an African American postal worker who had worked with the U.S. Postal Service for a number of years sought a promotion. According to the announcement, the successful candidate had to have "highly developed written and oral communication skills" and "well developed human relations skills." The screening panel consisted of three White males, although this composition violated the agency's policy. Sixteen persons applied for this promotion and of this total, twelve were White males, one was Latino, and three were African Americans. None of the African Americans made the top five after the prescreening. Elzie D. Odom, one of the African Americans who had considerable years of experience with the agency, complained, and he subsequently was given an interview. However, the job went to a White male and

Odom sued for race and age discrimination. A U.S. district court found that Odom indeed had been discriminated against, citing that he was better qualified and that his accomplishments were diminished in a written evaluation while the accomplishments of White applicants were highlighted. However, the Fifth Circuit Court of Appeals reversed the district court's decision (*Odom v. Frank*, 1993).

Extending the U.S. Supreme Court's decision in *McDonnell Douglas Corp. v. Green* (1973), the Fifth Circuit Court stated that:

> We also remain cognizant of the fact that the evaluation of applicants (and applications) for high level positions in any discipline—business, industry, government, military, or education—involves both objective and subjective elements. We also recognize that subjectivity has a potentiality for abuse by those evaluators who would use it to shield improprieties in the selection process, possibly even as a pretext for discrimination. On the other hand, as a general rule judges are not as well suited by training or experience to evaluate qualifications for high level promotion in other disciplines as are those persons who have trained and worked for years in the field of endeavor for which the applicants under consideration are being evaluated. Therefore, unless disparities in curricula vitae are so apparent as virtually to jump off the page and slap us in the face, we judges should be reluctant to substitute our views for those of the individuals charged with the evaluation duty by virtue of their own years of experience and expertise in the field in question. (*Odom v. Frank*, 1993, p. 847)

This standard, differences between and among minorities and Whites that slap one in the face, has been repeated in a number of cases (*Deines v. Texas Department of Protective and Regulatory Services*, 1999).

Clearly, the Fifth Circuit Court was saying that African Americans and other minorities have to accept some discrimination in American society and the law cannot redress all discrimination that occurs. It frankly acknowledged that subjective criteria could mask discrimination. Further, it is saying that in order to win a discrimination lawsuit, the judges have to be "slapped in the face." This means also that African Americans have to be substantially better than Whites to advance—a view that many African Americans have long held. To be equal or a little better is not good enough. An African American must be far better. Yet, Whites do not have to be far better or equal and can be a little lower in skills.

Differential Outcomes in Discrimination Cases

Although the standard in *McDonnell Douglas Corp. v. Green* applies to women, women, especially White women, may experience more favorable treatment than African Americans. Although this case comes from the Court of Appeals for the District of Columbia, the opinion referred to the U.S. Supreme Court's standard in deciding discrimination cases or *McDonnell Douglas Corp. v. Green*. This case involved two lawyers who worked for the Washington office of the American Dental Association (ADA). One official scheduled his retirement and both lawyers, one male and one female, applied for the opening. Reportedly, phrases from the White male's last evaluation were put in the job announcement to make him more qualified. The female lawyer, Carole Kolstad, contended that the White male lawyer was essentially preselected for the position and that she had no chance at the promotion. Kolstad met the initial requirements of standards established by *McDonnell Douglas*. Specifically, she was female, she applied for a position for which she was qualified, she was rejected, and another person was selected. When the burden shifted to the ADA, it countered that Kolstad lacked recent legislative experience and strong writing skills—experience and skills that the White male lawyer possessed. A jury and both the U.S. district court and court of appeals rejected this explanation, calling it a pretext for sex discrimination. Kolstad won her case and the only real dispute was whether she was entitled to punitive damages (*Kolstad v. American Dental Association*, 1997).

Admittedly, the Kolstad case occurred in another court of appeals, and it is not uncommon for a different law to emerge in a different part of the country. Generally, when there is a glaring contradiction in the laws, the U.S. Supreme Court takes a case from one of the circuits and decides the issue. However, this decision purportedly follows the U.S. Supreme Court's precedent in *McDonnell Douglas Corp. v. Green*. The real issue is whether Carole Kolstad's skills were so superior to the White male as to jump up and slap the jury and court in the face, which is the standard for African Americans.

But African Americans in the same D.C. Circuit have a more difficult time achieving justice. A year later in the court of appeals in Washington, an African American male's discrimination case was decided. While the issues were somewhat different from the Kolstad case, the decision provides some insight into racial discrimination cases. Darion M. Carney was an administrator at American University. He was named acting dean of students while the university searched for a permanent dean. Carney applied for the permanent position, but it eventually went to a White male. Carney then went back to his original job, director of student services. Later, his job was abolished, and Carney was forced to leave the university. He sued, contending that the university's failure to name him to the dean's position and the elimination of his director's job were discriminatory. However, the university won summary judgment in its favor, and the court of appeals ruled that Carney did not refute American's evidence of why he did not get the job (*Carney v. The American University*, 1998).

Three primary reasons were offered by American University for why Carney did not get the job—he did not do a good job as acting dean, he did not hold a doctoral degree, and he presented himself poorly during the interview. Of these three reasons, the only objective evidence that the court of appeals could acknowledge is that Carney did not have a doctoral degree, which it did (*Carney v. The American University*, 1998).

However, at major universities throughout the country, persons without doctorate degrees hold some administrative positions. In fact, the qualifying qualification is often a master's degree. American University implicitly suggested that this was the case because the job announcement stated that a doctoral degree was *preferred*. Thus, legitimately the White male who received the job offer could have been more qualified by holding a doctorate. At the same time, however, the White male could have had a master's degree, and Carney could have had a doctoral degree with the same results. Then, American University's position would have been that a doctoral degree was only preferred and that the White male was impressive during the interview and presented a strong vision for the dean's position. Then, the court of appeals, responding to Carney's argument that he had a doctoral degree and thus was entitled to the job, would have said that a doctoral degree was only preferred.

Another African American female sued her employer, George Washington University, a case which the court of appeals decided. Dr. Harriet Hunter-Boykin was hired as an assistant professor of Secondary Education in 1990. Dr. Hunter-Boykin subsequently learned that a White male hired during the same period was offered a tenure-track position at a higher salary. Dr. Hunter-Boykin's position was an untenured, lower-paid position. Dr. Hunter-Boykin's attorney notified George Washington University that he intended to bring a lawsuit in Dr. Hunter-Boykin's behalf alleging racial discrimination in hiring. A three-year statute of limitations existed for filing a lawsuit, and both parties agreed to suspend the starting of the clock while attempts were made to negotiate a settlement. However, negotiations failed, and George Washington University threatened to defend itself vigorously should a lawsuit be filed. A lawsuit was filed and George Washington University kept its promise.

George Washington University litigated the agreement to suspend the statute of limitations, arguing that Dr. Hunter-Boykin's lawsuit was filed several days too late. Over this trivial issue, a U.S. district court granted summary judgment in George Washington University's favor. However, the court of appeals reversed and ordered that Dr. Hunter-Boykin's lawsuit proceed (*Hunter-Boykin v. The George Washington University*, 1998).

During subsequent litigation, Dr. Hunter-Boykin could have or could not have prevailed. The legal database does not show what happened after the case was remanded to the lower court. In keeping with the theme of this book, this case shows that receiving justice is more difficult for African Americans. Clearly, social justice and fairness required that George Washington University correct this issue. It had a chance to avoid trial. Instead of making amends, it chose to put up a fight, which might have had the intention of frustrating Dr. Hunter-Boykin so that she would not want to work at George Washington University even if she won her case.

The only perceived justification for its initial decision in not offering Dr. Hunter-Boykin a tenured position is that she did not have her doctorate in hand at the time of her interview. Sometimes, candidates interview for jobs while completing their dissertations. They can receive job offers with the stipulation that they must finish their dissertations prior to the start of their employment. If they are not finished, they will start as lecturers or untenured teachers until they finish. Thereupon, they would be given tenure-track positions. Clearly, there is a problem if two people with the same credentials are hired at the same time, and the White male receives a tenure-track position with higher pay. Perhaps, if Dr. Hunter-Boykin was a White female, George Washington University or the initial federal court would not have treated her in this fashion.

Another African American female named Joyce A. Barbour in the Washington, DC, area sued her employer, the Environmental Protection Agency (EPA), because she had not been promoted as promised by her supervisor and because a White female had been given more rapid promotions. A jury found in Barbour's favor but the court of appeals reversed. The issue here was whether a fair comparison could be made between Barbour and her White colleague. Barbour, according to the EPA and the court of appeals, was responsible for only seven specific task management activities, but her White colleague had more numerous and more weighty tasks. Thus, a fair comparison could not be made between Barbour and her White colleague. Although the jury believed that it could make a comparison, the court of appeals said that a reasonable jury could not. Therefore, the verdict in Barbour's favor had to be reversed (*Barbour v. Browner*, 1999).

White plaintiffs alleging that African American administrators have discriminated against them seem to have their cases decided by a different legal standard. This case involved several White tenured law professors at the Thurgood Marshall School of Law at Texas Southern University, a predominately African American university. There seemed to be a long-running dispute between the mostly White law professors and the dean and associate dean of the law school. A vote of confidence was held and several professors indicated no confidence in the dean. A petition was sent to the president of the university to remove the dean. They filed a formal complaint with the American Bar Association regarding the dean's handling of the administration of the law school. Because of their activities, the White professors claimed that they received low merit raises that constituted racial discrimination and an attempt to punish them for exercising their free speech rights. Previously, these professors complained about the size of their merit raises and some adjustments were made for them.

Admittedly, the law school did not have a systematic evaluation policy, and an attempt was made to implement a new system for deciding merit raises. A system was devised in which professors rated themselves in several areas and forwarded their assessments to the associate dean. Then, the associate dean would agree or adjust the evaluation and forward this second-tier assessment to the dean, who would then decide on the merit raises. The three White plaintiffs contended that the associate dean lowered the point totals for all the White professors and raised the points for all the African American law professors. At the time of the trial, the three White professors were making $102,046, $98,297, and $97,332. They testified that they had been given teaching awards and had been at the school longer than most other law professors. According to them, comparable African American full law professors made on average $3,000 more than them as a result of the discrimination by the dean and associate dean. Highlighted in the decision were the White professors' years and rank in terms of salary. For instance, Eugene M. Harrington, whose salary was $102,046, had been at the law school the longest and was ranked seventh in salary. The case was decided before a magistrate and jury, which found in favor of the White professors. On appeal, the Fifth Circuit upheld the jury's decision but reversed as to the free speech issues.

A different legal standard appears to exist when White males contend that African American administrators have discriminated against them. The three White professors sued under the Civil Rights Act of 1871, Section 1981. The judges on the Fifth Circuit began by saying that the standard for White male plaintiffs alleging discrimination is the same standard that is used in Title VII cases as established by *McDonnell Douglas Corporation v. Green* (1973). However, the judges applied a different standard from what they had when African Americans or Latinos were plaintiffs. The White male plaintiffs did not show that the reasons given for their evaluations and pay raises were a pretext. Allegedly, the dean was accused of failing to give the White professors equal credit and consideration for their scholarship, research, community service, and publications. African American professors were said to be evaluated more favorably and thus received higher merit raises (*Harrington et al. v. Texas Southern University*, 1997). Missing from the decision was the African American administrators' reasons for why and how they evaluated these White professors, and the White plaintiffs' evidence that these reasons were a pretext for discrimination.

Maybe the dean and associate dean indeed engaged in discrimination against these White law professors. However, the issue here is the standard for making that decision and whether it differs from what African American plaintiffs must prove when they allege that White administrators have discriminated against them. Conceivably, a plausible explanation may be given for why the associate dean lowered the points of the White professors. For instance, longevity and teaching awards are not the basis for awarding merit raises in academia. Some professors' scholarly productivity goes down the longer these professors are on a job. There was nothing said about White law professors having more yearly scholarship than the African American law professors. The Fifth Circuit judges said that they were giving credence to the jury's decision and might have made a different decision if they had heard the case. The standard the judges used was whether a reasonable jury had enough evidence to make a decision in this case and they concluded that the jury did (*Harrington et al. v. Texas Southern University*, 1997).

However, three months before the Harrington case, the Fifth Circuit Court of Appeals reversed a jury's decision involving Tommy L. Swanson, an African American plaintiff, who sued his employer, the General Services Administration. The plaintiff, Swanson, sued alleging discrimination and retaliation. Almost chafing, the judges stated that "we once again address the nature and degree of evidence required to support a jury verdict in Title VII action alleging race discrimination and retaliation. . . . Following well-established precedent, we conclude that the evidence presented in this case was insufficient to support the verdict because Swanson failed to offer competent evidence suggesting either that GSA's non-discriminatory explanations were pretextual, or that illegal discrimination was a motivating factor notwithstanding the existence of a legitimate explanation" (*Swanson v. General Services Administration*, 1997, p. 1181). This certainly was not the standard used in deciding the Harrington case.

Probably, the Court of Appeals for the Fifth Circuit has been the bluntest in its view of racial discrimination in employment cases (i.e., a favorable decision or an African American requires evidence that jumps up and slaps judges in the face). Other circuit courts have not used this language, but they might have a similar standard that is not as bluntly stated. Given that African Americans tend to lose their lawsuits, it suggests that while other judges do not need to be slapped in the face, they utilize a standard that is very high for African Americans to overcome.

Notwithstanding, the Court of Appeals for the Fifth Circuit should be recognized for being honest in stating that some employment decisions may be tainted by racial discrimination, which may be hard to discern. Fairly applied, the law may be powerless to rectify all forms of discrimination. Typically, the law requires evidence to support one's case. A plaintiff may be correct in his or her allegations, but may not be able to prove the case. Without evidence, a plaintiff will lose. For instance, an interviewing panel or director can say that an African American applicant did not interview well, which is impossible for an African American to refute. The same is likely true if the contention is that an African American does not have good people skills. Unless an African American has won some awards for having good people skills, he or she is very likely to lose. Asking an applicant for a job or promotion what is his or her vision for the position may be the basis for a discriminatory decision. Two applicants fairly close in experience and education may receive different subjective evaluations regarding how each responded to a question regarding his or her vision for a particular position. The nature of employment decisions favors those who are making the decisions. Because these individuals tend to be White, African Americans can expect less justice. Although African Americans may be able to prevail and achieve justice, it will not come easily and will be more difficult to achieve.

Differential Adoption of Statistics in Discrimination Cases

Besides its decision in *McDonnell Douglas,* the U.S. Supreme Court has been hostile to the adoption of statistics in cases alleging racial discrimination. In a capital punishment case from Georgia, a study was conducted involving over two thousand cases. The researcher found overwhelming evidence that capital punishment was most likely to be meted out for defendants who have been convicted of killing White persons. As a result, African American defendants were denied equal protection of the law, which is guaranteed by the U.S. Constitution. However, the U.S. Supreme Court rejected the use of statistics to show racial discrimination and held that a defendant must specifically show that the officials in his or her case acted in a racial manner (*McCleskey v. Kemp*, 1987). This same logic has been used when African Americans have challenged unfair sentences involving crack cocaine and powder cocaine. In an employment case, the U.S. Supreme Court rejected use of statistics to show that minorities were tracked into lower-paid positions while Whites were given the higher-paid positions. Three dissenting members of this case contended that the Court had made establishing racial discrimination by statistical means more difficult and almost impossible to prove (*Wards Cove Packing Co. Inc. et al. v. Atonio et al.*, 1989).

Applying these views, one judge stated that a statistical study presented by African Americans in a class action lawsuit was meaningless. This case involved Metro-North Commuter Railroad, where Whites held most of the top jobs and African Americans had the lower-paid jobs. Also, African Americans argued that they were more likely to be disciplined than White employees. As part of the plaintiffs' lawsuit, a study was presented based on data supplied by Metro-North. The sociologist found that African Americans faced .7 disciplinary infractions and Whites faced .2. This constituted a disciplinary rate three and one-half times higher for African Americans. This difference was highly significant statistically, occurring less than 1 time in 10,000. Further, being African American reduced an employee's likelihood of being promoted by 33 percent. Metro-North hired its own research expert to counter the plaintiffs' study, who basically attacked the methodology used by the plaintiffs' expert and the conclusion that racial discrimination was present at Metro-North. Though Metro-North's research expert had access to the same data, he failed to conduct what he perceived as the proper methodology. In response to this criticism, the plaintiffs' researcher conducted additional analyses along the lines suggested by Metro-North's expert and still found racial discrimination. The plaintiffs' expert responded that Metro-North's expert essentially was attempting to explain away findings of racial discrimination. Although it was very obvious that the plaintiffs' expert had presented the soundest arguments, the judge demeaned the study and stated that it had proven nothing. The defense's statistical expert did not present a study that showed that racial discrimination had not occurred and only criticized what the plaintiffs' expert had done. According to the judge, he had grave reservations about the researcher's opinion that was "dressed in the garb of regression analysis" (*Robinson et al. v. Metro North*, 1998). Obviously, the judge did not understand the research and did not want to accept the study as valid.

Yet there does not seem to be uniformity in viewing statistics and numbers. Apparently, if African Americans present statistics, these statistics prove nothing much. However, if White plaintiffs present statistics to show that they have been discriminated against, these statistics carry more weight. Deciding a case of alleged discrimination against White law school applicants at the University of Texas, judges on the Fifth Circuit Court of Appeals seemed impressed with numbers and statistics. They stressed that the median grade point average (GPA) and Law School Admission Test (LSAT) scores for White applicants were 3.56 and 164, for African Americans 3.30 and 158, and for Latinos 3.24 and 157. The four White plaintiffs who were rejected for admission and sued the law school had GPAs of 3.8, 3.28, 3.13, and 2.98. The judges found these numbers, in addition to the selection process, probative of discrimination against these four White plaintiffs. Interestingly, only forty-one (8 percent) of the admitted students were African American and fifty-five (10.7 percent) were Latinos. Hence, Whites made up 81.3 percent of the admitted students and totaled about 513. African Americans and Latinos were blamed for taking up spaces that the four White plaintiffs deserved. It is just as plausible, and probably is more plausible, that some of the White students in the group of 513 had lower GPAs and LSAT scores than the four White plaintiffs (*Hopwood v. State of Texas*, 1996). Keeping in mind that Whites' median GPA was 3.56, which means that 50 percent of Whites had GPAs lower than 3.56, it is likely that White admitted students received admission with lower scores than African Americans and Latinos.

Other legal cases in the Eleventh and Fifth Circuits showed how the court viewed statistics and numbers submitted by persons who are not African American plaintiffs. These cases also show different standards utilized when the plaintiffs are African Americans and Whites or women. At one time, both women and minorities were denied opportunities to participate fully in the American workforce. Numerous jobs were reserved for White males. As cities and counties were sued and affirmative action plans implemented, some White males responded with lawsuits contending that they were the innocent victims of reverse discrimination. In reviewing these affirmative action plans, women and minorities splintered in separate directions.

To determine whether an affirmative action plan for African Americans was constitutional, the U.S. Supreme Court has mandated use of the strict scrutiny test, the highest and most difficult legal test to overcome (*Adarand Constructors, Inc. v. Pena*, 1995). In addition, general statistics regarding the composition of African Americans in a community and their composition in skilled positions are of little support for their case.

However, there is a different legal standard for women. Following a case in which the U.S. Supreme Court upheld the use of general statistics (*International Bd. of Teamsters v. United States*, 1977), the Eleventh Circuit Court of Appeals held that reliance upon general statistics is appropriate in gender-only cases when other anecdotal evidence exists (*Ensley Branch, NAACP v. Seibels*, 1994). For women, the legal test used for determining whether an affirmative action plan for them is constitutional is the intermediate legal test, a much easier test than the strict scrutiny test.

Also, general statistics about the percentage of women in the community and in skilled positions are probative. This difference between women and African Americans was highlighted in several cases. One case involved an affirmative action plan for women in the Dade County, Florida, Fire Department, where one judge wrote that it is easier to rule for women in affirmative action cases than racial minorities (*Danskine et al. v. Metro Dade County Fire Department*, 1999). Statistics showed that women made up 52 percent of Dade County but only 1 percent of the fire department workforce. The court determined that this evidence was probative. This was convincing evidence to support an affirmative action plan for women. However, similar statistics offered by African American plaintiffs would not be viewed equally. Although African

Americans could also show that they made up a significant percentage of citizens in Dade County and that stark racism kept them from holding jobs in the fire department, African Americans would not be treated the same as woman plaintiffs. African Americans have a more difficult legal burden to satisfy and a more difficult time achieving justice.

Conclusion

The Fifth Circuit Court of Appeals admitted that racial discrimination may exist in an employment decision that is masked by accepted subjective evaluations. In such situations, the courts are limited and unable to correct these discriminatory employment cases. Hence, racial discrimination cases that go to court resulting in adverse rulings or decisions against African American plaintiffs do not mean that the cases were without merit. However, the most significant aspect of this chapter is that there appears to be a double standard applied to African Americans, and this double standard is tougher for African Americans. Particularly, a White person alleging racial discrimination has an easier time prevailing in court than an African American alleging racial discrimination.

9

African Americans and Justice: Summary and Conclusions

THE THESIS OF THIS BOOK IS NOT that African Americans have a terrible life in America. It simply is that African Americans receive less justice—legal, social, educational, and economical. Moreover, African Americans have not received due appreciation for their military contributions, and this neglect implicates justice. Indeed, it is true that there is a declining significance of race (Wilson, 1980). This decline does not mean, however, that racial discrimination against African Americans has disappeared from society. Racially discriminatory eruptions frequently occur and appear in the media. For example, in 2004, Cracker Barrel Restaurants Corporation settled a lawsuit filed by the federal government to cease discrimination against African American customers. The company permitted a policy of allowing racist waitresses to switch or swap tables with other waitresses because these racist waitresses did not want to serve African Americans. Some Cracker Barrel restaurants also were accused of sitting all African American customers in the same area and referring to this section as the ghetto (Fear, 2004; Lichtblau, 2004). Of course, some individuals might view Cracker Barrel as a significant change because in the 1960s in Atlanta, Georgia, Lester Maddox, who later became the governor of Georgia, chased African Americans from his restaurant with pick ax handles, and then closed his restaurant rather than serve African Americans when ordered by the federal government.

A conservative African American in California, who believes that African Americans are too focused on race, wants to eliminate the collection of racial data in California. His simplistic view is that if there are no racial data, then

California departments and schools would not know the race of job applicants and students, and African Americans would not have data to accuse state officials of racial differences (Sanders, 2003). History and current policies tell us that this would not work. White Alabamians discovered means of disenfranchising African Americans without referring to their race in the early 1900s. Also, Texas may modify its 10 percent policy for admission to Texas colleges to aid upper-class Whites without referring to race. It is not that African Americans focus too much on race, but that Whites have not been able to give up their focus on race. This chapter summaries key points from some of the chapters and provides some concluding comments to explain the current state of affairs.

In chapter 1, several definitions were provided for justice and social justice. As stated, justice is the allocation of resources and burdens fairly. Further, to do justice means to act justly, to treat fairly or adequately, and to show due appreciation for. This initial chapter gives some historical background and shows the beginning of differential treatment for African Americans. It presents how the U.S. Supreme Court ruled one way for a Chinese group and a different way for African Americans on the essentially the same issue—equal protection of the laws. Declaring to be colorblind, some states systematically disenfranchised African Americans in the early 1900s without mentioning race, but the sole focus was race.

In chapters 2 and 7, the discussions involving students at the University of Wisconsin and applicants to the University of Texas illustrate critical points about affirmative action in colleges and universities. Undoubtedly, many Whites believe that they cannot get into college because African Americans are taking their seats because of affirmative action. African Americans constitute a very small percentage of students at White universities. As stated in chapter 7, the group that has gained the most from affirmative action is women, particularly White women. For the past few years, women have made up half and sometimes more than half of medical school, law school, and undergraduate students. But the false impression is given that the chief beneficiary of affirmative action is African Americans.

Chapter 5 shows the injustice toward African Americans who have served in the military and have not been given respect and due appreciation for their service. Money, land, and freedom were promised to slaves who fought in various military campaigns, but often, slaves received nothing. Further, this chapter contends that the differences in treatment between Jessica Lynch and Shoshona Johnson are typical of how African Americans have been slighted for their long military contributions.

As stated in chapters 1, 3, and 8, African Americans have had a difficult time achieving justice in the legal system. African Americans have experienced a few victories in the legal system, but more times than not, they have lost. This book asserts that even today that there is a double standard in law that disfavors African Americans. For instance, an affirmative action program for African Americans is judged legally by a higher and tougher legal standard than an affirmative action program for women. In 2003, the U.S. Supreme Court decided two cases involving diversity programs at the University of Michigan, and both cases were decided by strict scrutiny (*Gratz v. Bollinger*, 2003; *Grutter v. Bollinger*, 2003). The U.S. Supreme Court has permitted this tougher standard for African Americans, and there has not been an explanation for why or criticisms from the legal community.

Similarly, a double standard exists in the law regarding quotas. Quotas are legal in women's athletics but are not legal for African Americans in society. The reason for these double standards is that affirmative action for women benefits a large number of White females who are the nieces, sisters, daughters, daughters-in-law, and could-have-been-wives of primarily White male judges. When the judges are female, the reason is for some of the above factors and group interests. This is discussed more extensively in the Strolovitch study presented later in this chapter.

The sum of these chapters presents a veiled injustice for African Americans. Assertions like what Horowitz has made—African Americans have received numerous unjust benefits from the government, special laws, and affirmative action—fuel and stoke racism. It strains credulity to claim that 298 African American students out of a total of 6,341 persons intending to apply at the University of Texas are depriving White students of seats. Texas admitted that the number of minorities made this class more diverse than previously, which means that when *Hopwood* was decided, African Americans made up probably less than 5 percent of the students. Further, pointing to examples such as the 27 African American students with ACT scores between 16 and 20 while completely ignoring 429 White students with ACT scores between 16 and 20 and 6 White students with scores below 16 and 1 with a score of 10 is highly unfair and unjust. It is quite common for conservative Whites to say that African Americans are getting special benefits when it is not true. For Whites to say that African Americans receive a tremendous amount of benefits from affirmative action while knowing that this assertion is false is a very harmful injustice.

Critics of African Americans who condemn African Americans for discussing racism and race are disingenuous. Race and racism are an enduring part of American society. They are indelibly pressed into the fabric of society, which numerous Whites said in the late 1800s and early 1900s. They don't say that now, but it does not mean that racism has been erased. Conservative Whites in political campaigns frequently inject race, without mentioning it, to gather support for winning offices (Feld, 2003). The following discussions amplify latent consideration of race.

Recall that the Fifth Circuit Court of Appeals in *Hopwood v. the State of Texas* (1996) outlawed the use of race in admission decisions at the School of Law at the University of Texas. Conservatives hailed this decision and a goal of a colorblind society in which race is not an issue. The Texas legislature came up with the colorblind 10 percent rule, where the top 10 percent of each school or school district was eligible for admission to the University of Texas, as well as other Texas colleges and universities. But now, upper-class persons are upset with this rule because their children cannot get into the flagship universities in Texas, and support is increasing to change the 10 percent rule. Race was not a factor in the 10 percent rule. Now, colorblind and race-neutral Whites want a formula that increases their numbers at the University of Texas. Race will not be an explicit proposed change, but a factor will be proposed that correlates with being White and high social class. Regardless of what these Whites later say, they want race to be included in admission—particularly their race and social class.

Barry Feld (2003), a sociologist and law professor, discussed cogently the politics of race and juvenile justice and the effects of modern White racism on numerous institutions. Feld says that it is now politically incorrect to be openly a racist or to express racist thoughts. Thus, Whites have developed code words that have racial themes and are designed to invoke racism among Whites. Feld wrote that:

> Unfortunately, our public policy debates about poverty and inequality, the allocation of social resources and benefits, and welfare and crime have become intertwined with questions of race. Poor blacks who live in concentrated poverty are effectively segregated from the social, economic, and political mainstream and engage in behaviors of which the dominant culture disapproves. The mass media convey biased and misleading images that incite white viewers' fear and indignation and activate stereotypes and prejudices. Conservative politicians exploit voters' sensitivities to matters of race with coded messages that are designed to sustain a right-wing coalition and to promote racial animus. As a result, Americans engage in a subterranean discourse on race without confronting its reality. As long as the white public and politicians identify long-term poverty and its associated problems—unemployment, drug abuse, criminality, and illegitimacy—as a black condition that is separate from the mainstream of American society, policy makers can evade a sense of governmental responsibility or public obligation. (Feld, 2003, p. 796)

Dara Strolovitch (1998) provided statistical support for modern racism in her study of race, gender, and affirmative action. Strolovitch, using a national probability sample, studied attitudes toward support for antidiscrimination laws for women and African Americans. Often, many Whites say that they are opposed to governmental support because it violates American values of individualism and opposition to governmental activism. Strolovitch was able to incorporate these measures in her study, as well. She included a proxy of racism, which was the extent to which a respondent believed that African Americans were hard-working. She found that Whites are more supportive of affirmative action when it is perceived as benefiting Whites or White women and less supportive of affirmative action when it is perceived as benefiting African Americans. Specifically, 41 percent of White men were strongly in favor of antidiscrimination laws for African Americans but 51 percent of them were strongly in favor of antidiscrimination laws for women; 43 percent of White women were strongly in favor of antidiscrimination laws for African Americans but 69 percent of them were strongly in favor of antidiscrimination laws for women; 68 percent of African American men were strongly in favor of antidiscrimination laws for African Americans but 62 percent of them were strongly in favor of antidiscrimination laws for women; 77 percent of African American women were strongly in favor of antidiscrimination laws for African Americans but 70 percent of them were strongly in favor of antidiscrimination laws for women. These findings, according to Strolovitch, reflect group interests. A group is more likely to support a policy that favors its group as opposed to another group.

However, the data show more. African Americans are more in favor of antidiscrimination laws for African Americans and White women, but the opposite is true for Whites. That is to say, White females are opposed to discrimination against them, but they are less opposed to discrimination against African Americans. African Americans are against discrimination against them and are against discrimination against White females. Although Strolovitch did not highlight this point, her data say that both African American women and African American men are more opposed to social injustice and in favor of justice than White males and White females.

These data also show what Strolovitch called modern racism by Whites and declared that Whites play favorites. Strolovitch wrote that "by showing that discriminatory beliefs, individualism, and attitudes about the role of government are predictive of support for race-targeted anti-discrimination policy, but not support for gender-targeted polices, this study demonstrates that opposition to these programs is not simply the result of support for individual initiative and opposition to government activism. Instead, the results clearly show that some of the controversy surrounding anti-discrimination and affirmative action policies for blacks stem, at least in part, from the same discriminatory beliefs and practices that anti-discrimination policies are intended to combat" (Strolovitch, 1998, p. 44).

This modern racism explains several points. Returning to the issue of differential standards for discrimination in chapter 8, one can understand why these exist when Strolovitch's research is taken into account. In the Kolstad case, a white female lawyer won her case when the jury rejected the purported reasons for not promoting her—a lack of recent legislative experience and strong writing skills. The jury in this case, drawn from the District of Columbia, likely had a majority of African Americans. African Americans oppose discrimination more than Whites. Whites, including some White judges, are less opposed to discrimination when it applies to African Americans. Compounding this issue are the constant criticisms and falsehoods that African Americans have all this affirmative action and special laws, depriving more deserving Whites of jobs. These factors affect how discrimination cases are viewed and how the racial makeup of a jury and the legal system will view discrimination cases. If a White employer says that an African American did not get a job or promotion because the African American lacked strong writing skills, this assertion is more likely to be believed given that there are incessant comparisons of Whites' and African Americans' grade point averages, SAT scores, and LSAT scores.

Modern racism also likely will prevent African Americans from receiving reparations for slavery. The courts have indicated that the issue of reparations for African Americans is a political issue, not a legal one. The president or the executive branch and the Congress or the legislative branch would have to address this issue. Any White politician who advocates and votes for reparations for African Americans will quickly be defeated. President Clinton, who enjoyed considerable support from African Americans in his election, would not apologize for slavery because the vast majority of Whites, according to the polls, did not want him to apologize. These Whites believe that they have already paid by freeing the slaves and giving the descendants of slaves the Great Society programs and affirmative action.

Further, modern racism has become ingrained in public policy, making a reversal of public policy more difficult to change. For example, African Americans and others have pointed out the unfairness of incarcerating large numbers of African Americans for offenses like drug possession. Because of this "Get Tough" policy against African Americans, the country has experienced a boom in prison construction. These prisons have had some economic benefit to rural counties. More important, these inmates count in the counties in which they are incarcerated. This gives these rural counties more representation in state and federal Houses of Representatives and gives these counties more federal funding. The neighborhoods from which these inmates come receive less (Butterfield, 2004). In short, there are economic benefits to incarcerating large numbers of African Americans and these policies have become ingrained and difficult to change.

Then, institutional racism remains a current barrier, such as the differential treatment of Shoshana Johnson and Jessica Lynch. DeWayne Wickham (2003) gives an excellent example of this type of institutional White racism by criticizing how Hollywood intends to deal with the issue of the late Senator Strom Thurmond, a former segregationist who had championed the oppression of African Americans, and the late Senator Thurmond's African American illegitimate daughter. A Hollywood producer plans a movie but the heroine is not the African American, but a White reporter for the *Washington Post*. Wickham stated quite correctly that "Hollywood has a long history of turning the story of a black person's struggle into a celebration of some white person's deed . . . [and] Hollywood can't bring itself to make a movie about the harm that the bad acts of some white people had on a black person without leaning over backward to attach a white hero to the story" (p. 13A). As example, Wickham cites the movie *Cry Freedom*, about a Black South African who was killed in jail, the movie *Ghosts of Mississippi*, and the movie *Glory*. Furthermore, the character that Denzel Washington played in *Glory* was shown to have died at the end, but this African American soldier survived the charge against the fort (Wickham, 2003). White males are the heroes in all these movies.

In a similar fashion, White females are the heroines in the Jessica Lynch story and the story about Senator Strom Thurmond's African American daughter who loved her father and kept his secret. Along similar lines, Kimberly Peirce, a White female director, made a movie about the killing of Brandon Teena, a transsexual person who was killed in Nebraska by Tom Nissen and John Lotter. Nissen and Lotter raped Brandon after discovering that Brandon was anatomically a female and then decided to kill Brandon to eliminate Brandon as a witness. Hilary Swank played Brandon Teena and won best actress for her role in the move *Boys Don't Cry*. The movie showed two people that were killed—Brandon Teena, who was White, and Lisa Lambert, a White female. However, Phillip DeVine, an African American male, who was a friend of Lisa Lambert, also was killed in the house. Both Lisa Lambert and Phillip DeVine were killed simply because they were witnesses. The movie left the African American male out and gave viewers the impression that only two people were killed, when there were three people killed. The African American male was erased from the movie. In a time when society is supposed to be more sensitive to crime victims, and this sensitivity has been credited, in part, to the women's movement, it is amazing that Phillip DeVine was erased by a female writer and director. But given the modern racism in this society, Phillip DeVine's erasure is not amazing and continues a pattern that has been occurring for hundreds of years. Phillip's erasure violates and illustrates three of the types of justice espoused by Brady (1998) that were defined in chapter 1— commutative justice, communal justice, and social justice—and shows what African Americans endure today.

References

Adarand Constructors, Inc. v. Pena, 515 U.S. 200 (1995).

Alexander, R., Jr., (1996). African American youths and drugs: A time to pursue a mental health approach. *Journal of Black Psychology, 22,* 374–387.

Alexander, R., Jr. (1997). Juvenile delinquency and social work practice. In A. Roberts & C. A. McNeece (Eds.), *Social work policy and practices in the justice system* (pp. 181–197). Chicago, IL: Nelson-Hall.

Alexander, R., Jr. (2001). *To ascend into the shining world again.* Westerville, OH: Theroe Enterprises.

Alexander, R., Jr., & Gyamerah, J. (1997). Differential punishing of African Americans and Whites who possess drugs: A just policy or a continuation of the past. *Journal of Black Studies, 28,* 97–111.

Alt, W. E., & Alt, B. L. (2002). *Black soldiers, White wars: Black warriors from antiquity to the present.* New York: Praeger.

America, R. F. (2002). Reparations and public policy. In T. D. Boston (Ed.), *Leading issues in Black political economy* (pp. 305–311). New Brunswick, NJ: Transaction Publishers.

Arneson, R. J. (1993). Preferential treatment versus purported meritocratic rights. In S. M. Cahn (Ed.), *Affirmative action and the university: A philosophical inquiry* (pp. 157–164). Philadelphia, PA: Temple University Press.

Asseo, L. (1996, May 16). Federal supreme court makes it harder to charge racism. *Sentinel,* p. A1.

Atkinson, A. C. (Producer) (1998, November 29). *The black farmer.* 60 Minutes (Television).

Aubry, L. (2002, May 29). Urban perspective: Reparations; long-delayed and much maligned. *Los Angeles Sentinel,* p. A7.

Austin, A. (1995). The overrepresentation of minority youths in the California juvenile justice system: Perceptions and realities. In K. K. Leonard, C. E. Pope, & W. H. Feyerherm (Eds.), *Minorities in juvenile justice* (pp. 153–178). Thousand Oaks, CA: Sage.

Avery v. Georgia, 345 U.S. 559 (1953).

Barbour v. Browner, 181 F.3d 1342 (D.C. Cir. 1999).

Barclay, D. (2001a). AP peculiar land swaps leave Blacks with little of their ancestors' Georgia Island. Retrieved February 2, 2004, from http://www.mamiwata.com/swap.html.

Barclay, D. (2001b). Car dealer acquired Black farmers' land by foreclosing on loans. Retrieved February 2, 2004, from http://www.mamiwata.com/car.html.

Barclay, D., & Lewan, T. (2001). Developers and lawyers use a legal maneuver to strip Black families of land. Retrieved February 2, 2004, from http://www.mamiwata.com/lawyer.html.

Barclay, D., Lewan, T., & Breed, A. G. (2001). Landownership made Blacks targets of violence and murder. Retrieved February 2, 2004, from http://www.mamiwata.com/murder.html.

Barker, R. L. (2003). *The social work dictionary* (5th ed.). Washington, DC: NASW Press.

Basler, R. (1953). *The collected works of Abraham Lincoln, Volume 3.* New Brunswick, NJ: Rutgers University Press.

Batson v. Kentucky, 476 U.S. 79 (1986).

Bazyler, M. J. (2002). The Holocaust restitution movement in comparative perspective. *Berkeley Journal of International Law, 20,* 11–44.

Beauchamp, T. L. (1993). Quotas by any name: Some problems of affirmative action in faculty appointments. In S. M. Cahn (Ed.), *Affirmative action and the university: A philosophical inquiry* (pp. 212–216). Philadelphia, PA: Temple University Press.

Beck, E. M., & Tolnay, S. E. (1990). The killing fields of the deep south: The market for cotton and the lynching of Blacks, 1882–1930. *American Sociological Review, 55,* 526–539.

Beck, E. M., & Tolnay, S. E. (1995). Violence toward African Americans in the era of the white lynch mob. In D. F. Hawkins (Ed.), *Ethnicity, race, and crime: Perspectives across time and place* (pp. 121–144). Albany, NY: State University of New York Press.

Beck, J. (1998, July 16). When playing the race card backfires. *Chicago Tribune,* p. 21.

Belknap, M. R. (1987). *Federal law and southern order: Racial violence and constitutional conflict in the post-Brown south.* Athens, GA: The University of Georgia Press.

Bell, D. A. (1980). *Race, racism, and American law.* Boston, MA: Little, Brown.

Berea College v. Kentucky, 211 U.S. 45 (1908).

Black, L. D., & Black, S. H. (1985). *An officer and a gentleman: The military career of Lieutenant Henry O. Flipper.* Dayton, OH: The Lora Company.

Board of Regents v. Roth, 408 U.S. 564 (1972).

Bodner et al. v. Banque Paribas, 202 F.R.D. 370 (US Dist ED, NY 2000).

Bond, H. M. (1934). *The Education of the Negro in the American social order.* New York: Prentice-Hall.

Bond, J. (1998). Forward. In W. Feinberg (Ed.), *On higher ground: Education and the case for affirmative action* (pp. ix–x). New York: Teachers College, Columbia University.

Boyd v. Nebraska ex rel. Thayer, 143 U.S. 135 (1892).

Boyle, D. (2003). Book review & response: Unsavory White omissions? A review of uncivil wars. *West Virginia Law Review, 105*, 655–698.

Bradford, W. (2003). With a very great blame on our hearts: Reparations, reconciliation, and an American Indian plea for peace with justice. *American Indian Law Review, 27,* 1–175.

Brady, B. V. (1998). *The moral bond of community: Justice and discourse in Christian morality.* Washington, DC: George University Press.

Brandt, D. (1998/1999, Winter). Affirmative action for Whites at the University of Wisconsin. *Journal of Blacks in Higher Education, 22,* 127.

Bridges, G. S., Conley, D. L., Engen, R. L., & Price-Spratlen, T. (1995). Racial disparities in the confinement of juveniles: Effects of crime and community social structure on punishment. In K. K. Leonard, C. E. Pope, & W. H. Feyerherm (Eds.), *Minorities in juvenile justice* (pp. 128–152). Thousand Oaks, CA: Sage.

Bridges, G. S., & Steen, S. (1998). Racial disparities in official assessments of juvenile offenders: Attributional stereotypes as mediating mechanisms. *American Sociological Review, 63,* 554–570.

Brown v. Commonwealth, 144 Va. 676 (1926).

Brown v. Fordice, 157 F.3d 388 (5th Cir. 1998).

Brown v. Mississippi, 297 U.S. 278 (1936).

Browne, J. Z. (1998, June 11). ACLU to challenge Maryland state police over racial profiling. *Amsterdam News*, p. 4.

Bryan, C. W. (2003). Precedent for reparations? A look at historical movements for redress and where awarding reparations for slavery might fit. *Alabama Law Review, 54,* 599–616.

Bryant, A. (1998, May 13). 2 in Texaco case found not guilty. *New York Times*, p. A1.

Buckley, G., & Bolden, T. (2003). *American patriots: The story of Blacks in the military from the revolution to desert storm.* New York: Crown.

Bullock, H. A. (1967). *A History of Negro education in the south.* Boston, MA: Harvard University Press.

Bureau of Justice Statistics (1999). *Compendium of federal justice statistics, 1998.* Washington, DC: Author.

Butterfield, F. (2004, April 30). Study tracks boom in prisons and notes impact on counties, *New York Times*, A19.

Cahn, S. M. (1993). Introduction. In S. M. Cahn (Ed.), *Affirmative action and the university: A philosophical inquiry* (pp. 1–5). Philadelphia, PA: Temple University Press.

Campbell, B. (1995, April 16). Proportionality not right attack. *Times-Picayune*, p. C3.

Carney v. The American University, 151 F.3d 1090 (DC Cir. 1998).

Case, D. (2000, January 9). Roosevelt's rainbow held no pot of gold. *Syracuse Herald American*, p. B1.

Chambers et al. v. Florida, 309 U.S. 227 (1940).

Chambers, J. A. (1995). *Blacks and crime: A function of class.* Westport, CT: Praeger.

Chaney, R., & Carillo, K. (1999). Brutality against prisoners is a serious problem. In T. L. Roleff (Ed.), *Police brutality* (pp. 30–35). San Diego, CA: Greenhaven Press.

Civil Liberties Act of 1988, 50 U.S.C.S. Appx § 1989.

Claiborne, W. (1999, December 17). Disparity in school discipline found; Blacks disproportionately penalized under get-tough policies, study says. *Washington Post*, p. A3.

Clark v. Mayor, 29 Md. 277 (1868).

Clark, T. D. (1973). *The south since reconstruction*. Indianapolis, IN: Bobbs-Merrill.

Cobb v. The State, 218 Ga. 10 (1962).

Cobbs, A. S. (1991, July 1). Lincoln U. critics fear loss of Black heritage. *St. Louis Post-Dispatch*, p. A1.

Cohen, M. A. (2003). *Report on the racial impact of GMAC's finance charge markup policy*. Unpublished Manuscript.

College dropping swimming, diving. (1999, June 8). Associated Press Wire.

Collins, A. (1998). *Shielded from justice: Police brutality and accountability in the United States*. New York: Human Rights Watch.

Collins, S. (1999, October 3). School violence expert focuses on prevention. *New York Times*, p. B11.

Cooper, C., & Cannizaro, S. (1993, July 22). N.O. cops demanded Archie's murder. *Time-Picayune*, p. B1.

Corrigan et al. v. Buckley, 271 U.S. 323 (1926).

Corzine, J., Huff-Corzine, L., & Creech, J. C. (1988). The tenant labor market and lynching in the South: A test of split labor market theory. *Sociological Inquiry, 58*, 261–278.

Cox, J. (2002, February 21). Farmer-Paellmann not afraid of huge corporations. *USA Today*. Retrieved Febuary 13, 2004, from http://www.usatoday.com/money/general/2002/02/21/slave-activist.htm.

Craig-Taylor, P. (2000). Through a colored looking glass: A view of judicial partition, family land loss, and rule setting. *Washington University Law Quarterly, 78*, 737–778.

Cunningham v. Town of Narrows, 150 Va. 605 (1928).

D. L. Phillips and Wife, Louise E. Phillips v. R. M. Wearn, 37 S.E.2d 895 (1946).

Daniels, D. (1990, May 5). Vantage point: Reparations: A crucial issue for African Americans in the 90s. *Michigan Citizen*, p. 5.

Danskine et al. v. Metro Dade County Fire Department et al., 1999 U.S. Dist. LEXIS 12890.

Darboe, K. (2003). The impact of race relations in America of Dred Scott versus Sandford, Plessy versus Ferguson, and Brown versus Board of Education, Topeka, Kansas. *Great Plains Sociologist, 15*, 1–13.

DeFunis et al. v. Odegaard et al., 416 U.S. 312 (1974).

Deines v. Texas Department of Protective and Regulatory Services, 164 F.3d 277 (5th Cir. 1999).

Delaney, D. (1998). *Race, place, and the law 1836–1948*. Austin, TX: University of Texas Press.

DeLatte, L. W. (1994). The St. Landry riot: A forgotten incident of Reconstruction violence. In D. G. Nieman (Ed.), *Black freedom/white violence 1865–1900* (pp. 81–90). New York: Garland Publishing.

Department of Defense (2004). Statistical information analysis division. Retrieved April 20, 2004, from http://web1.whs.osd.mil/MMID/mmidhome.htm.

Derrick, A. (1999, June 2). No wonder black Americans shudder when the 'force' is on the loose. *Boston Globe*, p. A27.

Deutsch, L. (1999, October 14). A justice department official urges lawyers to help end racial profiling. *Sentinel*, p. A3.

Domanick, J. (1999, June 6). The state: A shooting reminiscent of the LAPD's worst days. *Los Angeles Times*, p. 6.

Downer v. Dunaway, 1 F. Supp. 1001 (M.D. Ga.) (1932).

Dred Scott v. Sandford, 60 U.S. 393 (1856).

D'Souza, D. (1995). *The end of racism: Principles for a multiracial society*. New York: Free Press.

Dugas, C. (1998, October 27). Nationwide's bias damages $100 million in Va. *USA Today*, p. B02.

Dunn, C. S., Cernkovich, S. A., Perry, R. L., & Wicks, J. W. (1993). *Race and juvenile justice in Ohio: The overrepresentation and disproportionate confinement of African American and Hispanic youth*. Bowling Green, OH: Bowling Green State University.

Durrette v. Commonwealth of Virginia, 201 Va. 735 (1960).

Dury et al. v. Neely et ux., 69 N.Y.S. 2d 677 (1942).

Edmonson v. Leesville Concrete Co., 500 U.S. 614 (1991).

Ellerton, D. (1998, March 26). School Watch Hyche appointment defended superintendent's turn: Clayton schools chief says 'only an idiot would play the race card.' *Atlanta Journal & Constitution*. p. J11.

Ensley Branch, NAACP v. Seibels, 31 F.3d 1548 (11th Cir. 1994).

Ex parte Mallory, 122 Va. 298 (1918).

Ex-aide claims N.J. governor sexually harassed him (2004, August 16). *USA Today*, p. 5A.

Fallon, S. (1999, August 29). Racial profiling protesters demand reforms. *The Sunday Record*, p. A3.

FBI lists caution signs for violence in classroom (September 7, 2000). *New York Times*, p. A20.

Fear, D. (2003, February 4). Draft bill stirs debate over the military, race and equity: Statistics on minorities' share of service's risks are disputed. *Washington Post*, p. A03.

Fear, D. (2004, May 4). Cracker Barrel, government settle discrimination suit. *Washington Post*, p. A02.

Federal Bureau of Investigation (2004). *Uniform crime report*. Retrieved from http://www.fbi.gov.

Federal Statute, 12 Statute 589 (1862).

Feinberg, W. (1998). *On higher ground: Education and the case for affirmative action*. New York: Teachers College, Columbia University.

Feld, B. C. (1995). The social context of juvenile justice administration: Racial disparities in an urban juvenile court. In K. K. Leonard, C. E. Pope, & W. H. Feyerherm (Eds.), Minorities in juvenile justice (pp. 66–97). Thousand Oaks, CA: Sage.

Feld, B. C. (2003). The politics of race and juvenile justice: The 'due process revolution' and the conservative reaction. *Justice Quarterly, 20*, 765–800.

Ferguson v. The State of Florida, 90 Fla. 105 (1925).

Feyerherm, W. H. (1995). The DMC initiative: The convergence of policy and research themes. In K. K. Leonard, C. E. Pope, & W. H. Feyerherm (Eds.), *Minorities in juvenile justice* (pp. 1–15). Thousand Oaks, CA: Sage.

Fikes v. Alabama, 352 U.S. 191 (1957).

Filbeck, K. (2003, January 27). Pentagon rebuts Rangel's race-based call for draft. *Human Events.* Retrieved April 30, 2004, from http://www.humaneventsonline.com/article.php?id=331.

Finnegan, L. J., Jr. (1999). Police brutality leads to a loss of trust in the police. In T. L. Roleff (Ed.), *Police brutality* (pp. 98–100). San Diego, CA: Greenhaven Press.

Fisher v. Hurst, 333 U.S. 147 (1948).

Flemming, J. (1976). *The Lengthening shadow of slavery: A historical justification for affirmative action for Blacks in higher education.* Washington, DC: Howard University Press.

Foner, J. D. (1974). *Blacks and the military in American history: A new perspective.* New York: Praeger Publishers.

Formwalt, L. W. (1994). The Camilla Massacre of 1868: Racial violence as political propaganda. In D. G. Nieman (Ed.), *Black freedom/white violence 1865–1900* (pp. 91–118). New York: Garland Publishing.

Francis, L. P. (1993). In defense of affirmative action. In S. M. Cahn (Ed.), *Affirmative action and the university: A philosophical inquiry* (pp. 9–47). Philadelphia, PA: Temple University Press.

Frazier, C. E., & Bishop, D. M. (1995). Reflections on race effects in juvenile justice. In K. K. Leonard, C. E. Pope, & W. H. Feyerherm (Eds.), *Minorities in juvenile justice* (pp. 16–46). Thousand Oaks, CA: Sage.

Fried, J. P. (1998). New charge against officers in the Louima case. *New York Times,* p. B10.

Furman v. Georgia 408 U.S. 238 (1972).

The Gallup Organization (1997). *Black/White relations in the U.S.: Findings show persistent gaps in perceptions of Blacks & Whites, though with substantial improvement over time.* Princeton, NJ: Author.

Garcia, M. (1997). The state of affirmative action at the threshold of a new millennium. In M. Garcia (Ed.), *Affirmative action's testament of hope: Strategies for a new era in higher education* (pp. 1–17). Albany, NY: State University of New York Press.

Garrett, C. (1997, October 17). In Dearborn: Firm accused of steering clients from Inkster homes. *Detroit News,* p. C3.

Gasner, C. (2004, February 4). Ginsburg recounts women's history in law. *The Crimson White,* p. 1.

Gavora, J. (1996, July 23). Quota system hurts team. *USA Today,* p. A14.

Gavora, J. (1998). You're in trouble again, Johnny. *Women's Quarterly, 14,* 4–8.

General Accounting Office (1995). *Equal Opportunity: DOD studies on discrimination in the military.* Washington, DC: Author.

Gent v. Cole, 38 Md. 110 (1873).

Get motivated. (2004, May 2). *Columbus Dispatch,* p. E16.

Glater, J. D. (2004, June 13). Diversity plan shaped in Texas is under attack. *New York Times,* pp. A1, A26.

Goering, R., & Wienk, R. (Eds.) (1996). *Mortgage lending, racial discrimination, and federal policy.* Washington, DC: Urban Institute Press.

Goldstein, A. (2004, August 7). Bush hits legacy college admissions. *Washington Post,* p. A08.

Gratz v. Bollinger, 539 U.S. 244 (2003).

Grutter v. Bollinger, 539 U.S. 306 (2003).

Guinn and Beal v. United States, 238 U.S. 347 (1915).

H. B. White v. Lewis White, 150 S.E. 531 (1929).

Haley v. Ohio, 332 U.S. 596 (1948)

Harlan, L. (1969). *Separate and unequal: Public school campaigns and racism in the southern seaboard states, 1901–1915.* Chapel Hill, NC: University of North Carolina Press.

Harrington et al. v. Texas Southern University, 118 F.3d 359 (5th Cir. 1997).

Harris, L. A. (2003). Reparations as a dirty word: The norm against slavery reparations. *University of Memphis Law Review, 33,* 409–448.

Hart v. Commonwealth, 131 Va. 726 (1921).

Hening's Virginia Statutes at Large, Volume 9, Chapter II, 1777.

Hennessey, M. M. (1994). Political terrorism in the Black Belt: The Eutaw riot. In D. G. Nieman (Ed.), *Black freedom/white violence 1865–1900* (pp. 157–170). New York: Garland Publishing.

Herrnstein, R. J., & Murray, C. (1994). *The bell curve: Intelligence and class structure in American life.* New York: Free Press.

Higginbotham, F. M. (2003). A dream deferred: Comparative and practical considerations for the Black reparations movement: Introduction: A dream revived: The rise of the Black reparation movement. *New York University Annual Survey of American Law, 58,* 447–455.

Holley, M. (1995, April 10). Tennis everyone, thanks to Barash. *Boston Globe,* p. 37.

Holmes, D. O. W. (1969). *The Evolution of the Negro College.* New York: Arno Press.

Holmes, S. A. (1997, November 23). A dilemma led to a deal over hiring tied to race. *New York Times,* p. 37.

Honadle v. University of Vermont & State Agri. College, 56 F. Supp 2d 419 (VA 1999).

Hopwood v. State of Texas, 78 F.3d 932 (5th Cir. 1996).

Horowitz, D. (2001, January 3). Ten reasons why reparations for Blacks is a bad idea for Blacks—and racist too. *FrontpageMagazine.com.* Retrieved April 12, 2004, from http://www.frontpagemag.com/Articles/ReadArticle.asp?ID=1153.

Horowitz, D. (2002). *Uncivil wars: The controversy over reparations for slavery.* San Francisco, CA: Encounter Books.

Horowitz, D. (2003). Book review & response: Unsavory Black insinuations: A reply to David Boyce. *West Virginia Law Review, 105,* 699–710.

Howard, J. R. (1997). Affirmative action in historical perspective. In M. Garcia (Ed.), *Affirmative action's testament of hope: Strategies for a new era in higher education* (pp. 19–45). Albany, NY: State University of New York Press.

Hudson, M. (1996). *Merchants of misery: How corporate America profits from poverty.* Monroe, ME: Common Courage Press.

Hudson, R. O. (2000, March 13). Profiling is part of pattern of some who abuse their badges. *St. Louis Post-Dispatch,* p. C7.

Hunter-Boykin v. The George Washington University, 132 F.3d 77 (DC Cir. 1998).

Hutchinson, E. O. (1999, May 25). Los Angles shooting—are Black women the new menace to society. *JINN Magazine.* Retrieved from http://www.pacificnews.org/jinn/stories/5.11/990525-black-women.html.

Ingram, C. (1997, April 10). Wilson proposes overhaul of juvenile justice system; politics; Governor presents 20 bills to get tough with violent youth crime, including a suggestion that the minimum age for death penalty be lowered to 14. *Los Angeles Times,* p. 3.

In re African-American Slave Descendants Litigation, 2004 U.S. Dist. LEXIS 872 (2004).

In re: Holocaust Victim Assets Litigation, 302 F. Supp. 2d 59 (US Dist ED, NY 2004).

In re Quong Woo, 13 F.2 29 (1882).

International Bd. of Teamsters v. United States, 431 U.S. 324 (1977).

Jack Arabas v. Thomas Ivers, Superior Court, A. D. (1784).

Jacobs, D., & Carmichael, J. T. (2002). The political sociology of the death penalty: A pooled time-series analysis. *American Sociological Review, 67,* 109–131.

Jacoby, T. (1999, April 18). Diallo's death and the costs of protest. *Washington Post,* p. B1.

James, J. B. (1984). *The ratification of the fourteenth amendment.* Macon, GA: Mercer University Press.

Jones, L. L. (1996). The myth of a racist criminal justice system. *American Journal of Criminal Justice, 20,* 277–280.

Jones, T. J. (1916). *A study of the private and higher schools for colored people in the United States.* Washington, DC: U.S. Department of the Interior.

Jordan, W. D. (1968). *White over black: American attitudes toward the negro 1550–1812.* Chapel Hill, NC: University of North Carolina Press.

Kaczorowski, R. J. (1985). *The politics of judicial interpretation: The federal courts, department of justice and civil rights, 1866–1876.* New York: Oceana.

Kauffman, A. H., & Gonzalez, R. (1993). The Hopwood case: What it says and what it doesn't. In M. Garcia (Ed.), *Affirmative action's testament of hope: Strategies for a new era in higher education* (pp. 227–247). Albany, NY: State University of New York Press.

Keeley Tatsuyo Hunter v. The Regents of the University of California, 190 F.3d 1061 (9th Cir. 1999).

Keister, L. A. (2000). Race and wealth inequality: The impact of racial differences in asset ownership on the distribution of household wealth. *Social Science Research, 29,* 477–502.

Kekes, J. (1993). The injustice of strong affirmative action. In S. M. Cahn (Ed.), *Affirmative action and the university: A philosophical inquiry* (pp. 144–156). Philadelphia, PA: Temple University Press.

Kolstad v. American Dental Association, 108 F.3d 1431 (DC Cir. 1997).

Larson, C. J. (1988). The myth of a racist criminal justice system. *International Journal of Offender Therapy and Comparative Criminology, 32,* 176–177.

Lavine, E. H. (1930). *The third degree: A detailed and appalling exposé of police brutality.* New York: The Vanguard Press.

The legacy of Plessy. (1996, May 18). *Detroit Free Press,* p. C5.

Legal gerrymandering. (1997, March 7). *New York Times*, p. A37.

Leonard, K. K., & Sontheimer, H. (1995). The role of race in juvenile justice in Pennsylvania. In K. K. Leonard, C. E. Pope, & W. H. Feyerherm (Eds.), *Minorities in juvenile justice* (pp. 98–127). Thousand Oaks, CA: Sage.

Lewan, T. (2001a). With help from their white lawyer, a Black Mississippi family loses a farm. Associated Press. Retrieved February 9, 2004, from http://www.mamiwata.com/dealer.html.

Lewan, T. (2001b). Taking away the vote—and a Black man's land. Associated Press. Retrieved February 2, 2004, from http://www.mamiwata.com/vote.html.

Lewan, T., & Barclay, D. (2001, December 2). Torn from the land: Black Americans' farmland taken through cheating, intimidation, even murder. Associated Press. Retrieved February 2, 2004, from http://www.commondreams.org/headline011202-03.htm.

Lewis, R. M., & Patram, S. (1998). The pendulum swings: Affirmative action and recent Supreme Court decisions. *Journal of Research on African American Men, 9*, 43–62.

Lichtblau, E. (1999, April 16). Reno seeks easing of police tensions. *Los Angeles Times*, p. 8.

Lichtblau, E. (2004, May 4). Cracker Barrel agrees to plan to address reports of bias. *New York Times*. Retrieved May 5, 2004, from http://www.nytimes.com/2004/05/04/politics/04DISC.html.

Lindenmeyer, O. (1970). *Black & brave: The Black soldier in America*. New York: McGraw-Hill.

Livington, Jr., C. L. (1996). Affirmative action on trial: The retraction of affirmative action and the case for its retention. *Howard Law Journal, 40*, 145–204.

Lovett, B. L. (1994). Memphis riots: White reaction to Blacks in Memphis, May 1865–July 1866. In D. G. Nieman (Ed.), *Black freedom/white violence 1865–1900* (pp. 207–231). New York: Garland Publishing.

Lower-Basch, E. (2000). *TANF "leavers," applicants, and caseload studies: Preliminary analysis of racial differences in caseload trends and leavers outcomes*. Washington, DC: Office of the Assistant Secretary for Planning and Evaluation.

Marquis, J. (1998, August 26). Liposuction doctor has license revoked. *Los Angeles Times*, p. 21.

Marx, G. (1998, February 11). Young killers remain well-publicized rarity: 'superpredators' fail to grow into forecast proportions. *Chicago Tribune*, p. 1.

Massachusetts launches racial profiling probe (2004, May 5). *CNN.com*. Retrieved May 5, 2004, from http://www.cnn.com/2004/US/Northeast/05/05/racial.profiling.ap/index.html.

Mathews, J. (1990, October 2). Bias against Asians found in admissions to UCLA. *Washington Post*, p. A5.

Mauro, T. (1998, December 8). Court defends clerk hiring practices. *USA Today*, p. 1A.

Mayer, C. E. (1997, April 9). Minorities said to face bias in house hunting: Study finds Blacks, Hispanics treated worse. *Washington Post*, p. C9.

Mayer, C. E. (2003, October 1). Car-loan rates marked up more for Blacks, report says. *Washington Post*, EO1.

Mayer, C. E. (2004, January 31). GMAC agrees to settle racial-bias lawsuit. *Washington Post*, Retrieved February 11, 2004, from http://www.detnews.com/2004/autosinsider/0401/31/autos-51136.htm.

McCarthy, S. J. (1999). The use of extreme force is sometimes justified. In T. L. Roleff (Ed.), *Police brutality* (pp. 41–43). San Diego, CA: Greenhaven Press.

McCleskey v. Kemp, 481 U.S. 279 (1987).

McDonnell Douglas Corp. v. Green, 411 U.S. 792 (1973).

McQueen, A. (2000, April 26). Report finds juvenile system offers justice only for some: Policies and practices show racial disparities, civil rights reports says. *USA Today*, p. 6A.

Meredith, J. (2000, March 31). Capitol Hill hears Highland Park racial-profiling allegations. *Chicago Tribune*, p. 2D 11.

Meyer, F. A. (1989). The myth of a racist criminal justice system. *Policy Studies Review, 8*, 731–733.

Miller, J. G. (1996). *Search and destroy: African American males in the criminal justice system*. Cambridge, England: Cambridge University Press.

Minneapolis and St. Louis Railway Company v. Beckwith, 129 U.S. 26 (1889).

Missouri ex rel. Gaines v. Canada, 305 U.S. 337 (1938).

Mooney, B. C. (1998, February 28). Race card is misplayed in Roxbury. *Boston Globe*, p. B3.

Murray, C. A. (1984). *Losing ground: American social policy, 1950–1980*. New York: Basic Books.

Muwakkil, S. (1998, July 20). The sequel of that tainted 'race card' deck. *Chicago Tribune*, p. 13.

Myers et al. v. Anderson, 238 U.S. 368 (1915).

Niebuhr, R. (1965). *Mississippi black paper*. New York: Random House.

Northwest Civil Association v. Shelton, 27 N.W.2d 36 (Mich. 1947).

Odom v. Frank, 3 F.3d 839 (5th Cir. 1993).

Ogletree, C. J., Jr. (2003). Repairing the past: New efforts in the reparations debate in America. *Harvard Civil Rights–Civil Liberties Law Review, 38*, 279–320.

Oldenquist, A. (1993). Remarks on affirmative action. In S. M. Cahn (Ed.), *Affirmative action and the university: A philosophical inquiry* (pp. 189–196). Philadelphia, PA: Temple University Press.

Owens, T. (1994). *Lying eyes: The truth behind the corruption and brutality of the LAPD and the beating of Rodney King*. New York: Thunder's Mouth Press.

Pan, P. P. (1998, March 29). Tougher youth laws examined; in Md, It's unclear if prison is effective. *Washington Post*, p. B1.

Parish, N. (1998, June 9). HUD says firm wouldn't sell home to black couple, Jefferson County developer faces fine, other sanctions owners contest bias charge. *St. Louis Post-Dispatch*, p. A1.

Parker, K. (1998, April 5). Gender quota follies. *Denver Post*, p. G3.

Patterson v. Alabama, 294 U.S. 600 (1935).

Perkins v. Trustees of Monroe Avenue Church of Christ, 70 N.E. 2d 487 (Oh. 1946).

Peterson, K. S. (1998, September 29). Public clamors: Get tough at a tender age. *USA Today*, p. D10.

Phipps, M. B. (2001, August 17). Reparations for slavery. *Washington Afro-American*, p. A1.

Platt, A. M. (1997). The Rise and Fall of Affirmative Action. *Notre Dame Journal of Law, Ethics & Public Policy, 11*, 67–78.

Plessy v. Ferguson, 163 U.S. 537 (1896).

Poe, J. (1998, July 5). Race in the workplace: An intimate chronicle of one woman's experiences in corporate America. *Chicago Tribune*, 6.

Pope, C. E. (1995). Equity within the juvenile justice system: Directions for the future. In K. K. Leonard, C. E. Pope, & W. H. Feyerherm (Eds.), *Minorities in juvenile justice* (pp. 201–216). Thousand Oaks, CA: Sage.

Population Resource Center (2004). Executive summary: A demographic profile of Hispanics in the U.S. Retrieved May 4, 2004, from http://www/prcdc.org/summaries/hispanics/hispanics.html.

Porter, P. (2000, April 25). Nationwide settles suit on redlining. *Columbus Dispatch*, p. 1A.

Powers v. Ohio, 499 U.S. 400 (1991).

Powers, S. (1998, December 9). The gender trends: The law requiring gender equity in college sports has been called both a blessing and a curse, but OSU has embraced it. *Columbus Dispatch*, p. 7A.

Presley v. Etowah County Commissioner et al., 502 U.S. 491 (1992).

Race differences in discipline. (1999, December 27). *San Francisco Chronicle*, A22.

Rachels, J. (1993). Are quotas sometimes justified. In S. M. Cahn (Ed.), *Affirmative action and the university: A philosophical inquiry* (pp. 217–222). Philadelphia, PA: Temple University Press.

Raine, W. J. (1967). *Los Angeles riot study: The perception of police brutality in South Central Los Angeles.* Los Angeles, CA: Institute of Government and Public Affairs.

Rankin, B. (1999, August 11). Black lawyers urge Rehnquist to ditch tune ABA: 'Dixie.' *The Atlanta Constitution*, p. A4.

Ratliff v. Beale, 20 So. Rep. 865 (Miss. 1896).

Rawls, J. (1971). *A theory of justice.* Cambridge, MA: Harvard University Press.

Reed, C. (1996, May 15). Supreme Court rejects 'unfair to blacks' defence [*sic*] in crack cocaine appeals. *Guardian*, p. 110.

Regents of the University of California v. Bakke, 98 S. Ct. 2733 (1978).

Ritter, R. (1996). The Decatur federal case: A summary report. In J. Goering & R. Wienk (Eds.), *Mortgage lending, racial discrimination, and federal policy* (pp. 445–450). Washington, DC: Urban Institute Press.

Robinson et al. v. Metro-North, 1998 U.S. Dist. LEXIS 373 (S.D. NY).

Robinson, R. (2001). *The debt: What America owes to Blacks.* New York: Plume.

Ross, S., & Yinger, J. (2002). *The color of credit: Mortgage discrimination, research methodology, and fair-lending enforcement.* Cambridge, MA: The MIT Press.

Sanders, J. (2003, June 26). Connerly's crusading is paying off. *The Sacramento Bee.* Retrieved September 6, 2004, from http://www.sacbee.com/content/politics/story/6923904p-7873237c.html.

Sandvik, A. (1999, March/April). The legacy of the G. I. Bill. *Minnesota: University of Minnesota Alumni Association*, p. 30.

Sawyers, A. (1989). Lincoln University: A study in separation. *Detroit News*, p. D1.

Schevitz, T. (2003, November 10). Women outnumber men for 1st time among medical school applicants. *San Francisco Chronicle*, p. A20.

Schroering, D. (2003, December 1). More women choosing law school at U. Kentucky. *Kentucky Kernel.*

Schubert, F. N. (2003). *Voices of the buffalo soldier: Records, reports, and recollections of military life and service in the west.* Albuquerque, NM: University of New Mexico Press.

Schuld, K. (1998). Look who's losing. *Women's Quarterly, 14,* 6.

Settlement may avert affirmative action test: rights groups help pay for deal to keep case out of Supreme Court. (1997, November 21). *Chicago Tribune,* p. 1.

Shelley et ux. v. Kraemer et ux., 68 S. Ct 836 (1948).

Shepardson, D. (1997, October 20). Special: public safety; Wayne courts get tough on juveniles. *Detroit News,* p. D1.

Simmons, R. (1982). *Affirmative action: Conflict and change in higher education after Bakke.* Cambridge, MA: Schenkman.

Sipuel v. Board of Regents of the University of Oklahoma, 332 U.S. 631 (1948).

Slocum, A. A. (1993). Strict scrutiny: The law and its special favorites. In M. Garcia (Ed.), *Affirmative action's testament of hope: Strategies for a new era in higher education* (pp. 205–226). Albany, NY: State University of New York Press.

Smith v. The University of Washington Law School, 2 F.Supp 1324 (W.D. WA. 1998).

Societe Nationale Industrielle Aerospatiale v. United States, 482 U.S. 522 (1987).

Son of Detroit mayor files complaint after being stopped by police. (1999, July 19). *Jet,* 54–55.

Soule, S. A. (1992). Populism and Black lynching in Georgia, 1890–1900. *Social Forces, 71,* 431–449.

Sparkman, J. (2003, January 22). Rangel race card on draft not backed up by data. *ChronWatch.* Retrieved from http://www.chronwatch.com/featured/contentDisplay .asp?aid=1365.

Spruill v. The North Carolina Mutual Life Insurance Company, 46 N.C. 126 (1853).

Squires, G. D. (2003). Racial profiling, insurance style: Insurance redlining and the uneven development of metropolitan areas. *Journal of Urban Affairs, 25,* 391–410.

Starr, B. (2003, June 18). Details emerge on Lynch convoy ambush. *CNN.com.* Retrieved May 2, 2004, from http://www.cnn.com/2003/US/06/17/sprj.irq.lynch.convoy/ index.html.

Statute at Large of South Carolina, Volume 7, Chapter 278, 1708.

Stone, C. (1999, April). Race, crime, and the administration of justice. *National Institute of Justice Journal,* 26–32.

Strauder v. West Virginia, 100 U.S. 303 (1880).

Strausberg, C. (1998, January 31). Flowers says it's time to get tough with youth offenders. *Chicago Defender,* p. 10.

Streib, V. L. (1987). *Death penalty for juveniles.* Bloomington, IN: Indiana University Press.

Strolovitch, D. Z. (1998). Playing favorites: Public attitudes toward race-and gender-targeted anti-discrimination policy. *NWSA, 10*(3), 27–53.

Suffolk University Law School (2004). Admissions profile for the entering class of 2003. Retrieved June 1, 2004, from http://www.law.suffolk.edu/admiss/facts.html.

Suro, R. (1997, May 8). White House, hill GOP offer get-tough measures on juvenile crime. *Washington Post,* A4.

Suro, R. (1999, April 16). Reno moves against police brutality, bias. *Washington Post,* A6.

Swanson v. General Services Administration, 110 F.3d 1180 (5th Cir. 1997).

Sweatt v. Painter et al., 339 U.S. 629 (1950).

Thompson v. Commonwealth, 131 Va. 847 (1921).

Timberg, C. (1999, July 22). Sing-along strikes a sour note; Chief Justice's selection of 'Dixie' distasteful, some say. *Washington Post*, p. B1.

Tolnay, S. E., & Beck, E. M. (1995). *A festival of violence: An analysis of Southern lynchings, 1982–1930.* Urbana and Chicago: University of Illinois Press.

Tolnay, S. E., Beck, E. M., & Massey, J. L. (1992). Black competition and white vengeance: Legal execution of Blacks as social control in the Cotton South, 1890 to 1929. *Social Science Quarterly, 73,* 627–644.

Truby, M. (1999a, May 27). Youth crime law under review: Oakland judges rule provision for sending juveniles to adult prison unconstitutional. *Detroit News*, p. D4.

Truby, M. (1999b, April 22). Ruling challenges youth law: For second time in six weeks, judge finds 97 juvenile sentencing law unconstitutional. *Detroit News*, p. D1.

Truby, M. (1999c, May 4). Adult prison for kid criminals? Case of honor student turned bank robber tests a controversial '87 juvenile crime law. *Detroit News*, p. A1.

Turner, K. B. (1998). African Americans and affirmative action in policing: A legal and historical analysis. *Journal of Research on African American Men, 9,* 95–110.

United States v. Price et al., 383 U.S. 787 (1966).

United States v. Virginia et al., 518 U.S. 515 (1996).

University et al. v. Cambreling, 14 Tenn. 78 (1834).

University of Alabama moves to acknowledge slavery links (2004, April 16). *CNN.com.* Retrieved from http://www.cnn.com/2004/EDUCATION/04/16/alabama/slavery .ap/index.html.

Venable v. A/S Forenede Dampskibsselskab, 275 F.Supp 591 (ED VA, 1967).

Village of University Heights et al. v. Cleveland Jewish Orphans' Home, 20 F. 2d 743 (6th Cir. 1927a).

Village of University Heights et al. v. Cleveland Jewish Orphans' Home, 275 U.S. 569 (1927b).

Walker, R. (1997, May 22). Landlord sued for racial discrimination. *Call & Post*, p. A1.

Walker, S., Spohn, C., & DeLone, M. (1996). *The color of justice: Race, ethnicity, and crime in America.* Belmont, CA: Wadsworth.

Walston, C. (1997, June 22). Battling 'lock 'em up' get tough alternatives: State caseworkers for youth offenders work with special programs to keep teens out of jail. *The Atlanta Journal*, p. G8.

Wansley v. Commonwealth of Virginia, 205 Va. 419 (1964).

Wards Cove Packing Co. Inc. et al. v. Atonio et al., 490 U.S. 642 (1989).

Washington Afro-American (1999). Police brutality results in a loss of respect for the police. In T. L. Roleff (Ed.), *Police brutality* (pp. 101–103). San Diego, CA: Greenhaven Press.

Whip v. State, 143 Miss 759 (1926).

White, W. F. (1948). *A man called White.* New York: The Viking Press.

Whittaker, C. E. (1997, April 22). Title IX 'message' delivered. *Atlanta Constitution*, p. F1.

Wickham, D. (2003, December 30). Thurmond's daughter deserves top movie billing. *USA Today*, p. 13A

Widespread redlining exposed. (1998, August 20). *Amsterdam News*, p. 30.

Wilbanks, W. (1985). Is violent crime intraracial? *Crime and Delinquency, 31,* 117–128.

Wilbanks, W. (1987). *The myth of a racist criminal justice system.* Monterey, CA: Brooks/Cole.

Williams v. Mississippi, 170 U.S. 213 (1898).

Williams, S. (2004, February 1). Filers pay for fast refunds. *Columbus Dispatch*, pp. D1, D2.

Williams, W. (1998, December 2). The civil war wasn't about slavery. *Jewish World Review.*

Wilson, R. (1994). The participation of African Americans in American higher education. In M. J. Justiz, R. Wilson & L. G. Björk (Eds.), *Minorities in higher education* (pp. 195–209). Phoenix, AZ: Oryx Press.

Wilson, W. J. (1973). The significance of social and racial prisms. In P. I. Rose, S. Rothman, & W. J. Wilson (Eds.), *Through different eyes: Black and White perspectives on American race relations* (pp. 395–409). New York: Oxford University Press.

Wilson, W. J. (1980). *The declining significance of race: Blacks and changing American institutions.* Chicago, IL: University of Chicago Press.

Wise, T. (2001). School shootings and White denial. AlterNet. Retrieved October 31, 2004, from http://www.altenet.org/story/10560.

Wolf, R. (1999, May 4). States act after school shootings, some focus on prevention; others pass get-tough laws. *USA Today*, p. A3.

Wolf-Devine, C. (1993). Proportional representation of women and minorities. In S. M. Cahn (Ed.), *Affirmative action and the university: A philosophical inquiry* (pp. 223–232). Philadelphia, PA: Temple University Press.

Wolfgang, M. E. (1970). *Crime and race: Conceptions and misconceptions.* New York: Institute of Human Relations Press.

Woodards, W., & Brand-Williams, O. (2000, February 9). Dearborn tracks race, tickets: Records of racial group, gender of stopped drivers shows that most are White males. *Detroit News*, p. D1.

Wooden v. Board of Regents of the Univ. Sys. of Georgia, 32 F Supp. 2d 1370 (SD GA, 1999).

Wordes, M., & Bynum, T. S. (1995). Policing juveniles: Is there bias against youths of color? In K. K. Leonard, C. E. Pope, & W. H. Feyerherm (Eds.), *Minorities in juvenile justice* (pp. 47–65). Thousand Oaks, CA: Sage.

Yick Wo v. Hopkins, 118 U.S. 356 (1886).

Zuckerman, D. (1999). Research on teen violence: Classroom killers and teen suicide. *National Center for Policy Research for Women & Families.* Retrieved October 31, 2004, from http://www.center4research.org/violenceb.html.

Zweig, R. W. (2001). *German reparations and the Jewish world: A history of the claims conference* (2nd ed.). Portland, OR: Frank Cass.

Index

About the Author

Dr. Rudolph Alexander Jr. holds an A.S. degree in criminal justice from Armstrong State College (now Armstrong State Atlantic University), a B.S. in criminology and corrections from Sam Houston State University, a Master's in social work from the University of Houston, and a Ph.D. in social work from the University of Minnesota. Since 1989, he has been on the faculty in the College of Social Work at Ohio State University, becoming a full professor in 2000. Dr. Alexander has published over fifty articles in peer-reviewed journals in social work and criminal justice. In addition, he has published four books: *Understanding Legal Concepts that Influence Social Welfare Policy and Practice* (2002), *Counseling, Treatment, and Intervention Methods with Juvenile and Adult Offenders* (2000), *Race and Justice* (2000), and his autobiography *To Ascend into the Shining World Again.* Dr. Alexander's current research focuses on the impact of prisoners upon grants to counties.